Wine Spectator's

Essentials
of Wine

A Guide to the Basics

HARVEY STEIMAN

Wine Spectator Press
a division of M. Shanken Communications, Inc., New York

9 8 7 6 5 4 3 2 1
Digit on the right indicates the number of this printing

ISBN 1-881659-61-5

Published by M. Shanken Communications, Inc.
387 Park Avenue South
New York, NY 10016

Distributed by Running Press Book Publishers
125 South Twenty-second Street
Philadelphia, PA 19103-4399

For subscriptions to *Wine Spectator*, please call:
(800) 752-7799 in the U.S. and Canada, or write:
PO Box 37367   Boone, IA 50037-0367
Visit our Web site at: www.winespectator.com

Preface

If you have never read a wine book before, this one should be your first. And even if you have, you'll want to check this one out anyway. It contains all you need to know to begin—or continue—a life-long love affair with the world's most complex and satisfying beverage.

We have tried to provide a definitive yet opinionated guide to the wide world of wine. You'll explore here all the major wine-producing regions from France to California, learn about the most important wine varieties, and find useful information about buying wine, storing your bottles and matching wine with food.

What makes the book special is the authority, knowledge and style of its author, Harvey Steiman. Harvey has been writing about wine for more than 25 years. A member of the *Wine Spectator* senior staff since 1984, his assignments have spanned almost every conceivable subject, including extensive travel pieces and tasting reports. He has visited the world's great vineyards and interviewed many leading wine producers. And he shares his expertise on food in the monthly menus he creates for the magazine.

Throughout *Essentials of Wine*, you'll enjoy the same straightforward, lively writing that *Wine Spectator* readers have come to expect from Harvey. He's more likely to use an analogy from music or sports than typical wine jargon.

Once you fall in love with wine, there is no end to the pleasure and interest it provides. So savor this book next weekend or on your next vacation. Let it help you expand your enjoyment of wine. That's what it's for, after all.

Marvin R. Shanken
Editor and Publisher,
Wine Spectator

Contents

The First Questions

Wine has things going for it that set it apart. Since Old Testament times, wine has been a vital part of human culture, possibly because of its magical ability to capture and preserve the fleeting tastes of sweet grapes, the essence of the sun that ripens them and the earth that grows them. It has other attributes. Its flavors enhance food. It has just enough alcohol to lubricate conversation and conviviality at the table. Wine is a social beverage, best appreciated with friends and family. It makes dinner more civilized. It slows us down a little, gives us something special to add to the moment.

On the other hand, wine is getting to be expensive. It can also seem complicated. Why bother learning all those regions and types, sorting out all those producers' names? Well, one great thing about wine is its amazing diversity. There are so many different wines from so many places in the world, and a little learning can introduce you to many of them. Also, knowing something about wine can get you more for your money and help you locate the best choices on a fancy restaurant's formidable wine list.

How to know what you like

Information, however, can only take you so far. The best way to learn about wine is to uncork a few bottles and start sampling. Take every opportunity to taste. It's fun, and it's the only way to determine what you like and what you don't. Once you can take a sip and say (to yourself, even if you don't say it out loud), "I like the wine because . . ." you open the door to a whole new world.

I, for example, tend to like smooth-textured wines with character. I always look for intensity of flavor, persistence of that flavor on the finish and the sort of balance that allows it all to come through without becoming overbearing or harsh. As a change of pace, I might appreciate a bracingly tart wine, but not as a steady diet. I have friends who love those tart wines. For them, something is missing if a wine does not tingle with acidity.

The only way to know what to buy is to taste and remember. Ideally, taste every wine before you buy it. Sometimes that's not possible, in which case knowing your preferences makes it possible to interpret what reviewers say in an entirely new light.

Memorable bottles can change your whole attitude toward wine. Some years ago, I invited a group of about two dozen friends to celebrate my birthday. I served a decent red and a white with the food. I also had just bought a case of good Champagne at a time when I really could not afford it. We expected the Champagne to last awhile. When my wife pulled the cork on a bottle and offered it, most of the guests seemed reluctant to take a glass. "Oh, I don't really like Champagne, but I'll have a glass to toast Harvey's birthday," they said. After the party, my wife remarked on how she looked forward to drinking more of the bubbly. "No such luck," I responded. "They drank it up." They all thought they didn't like Champagne, but they clearly had never experienced a good one. I created about 20 new Champagne drinkers that day.

When to drink it

Unlike wine, most food and drink are the same today as they were last week. A pint of fancy ice cream, for example, should look, feel and taste pretty much the way it did the last time you bought it, and it will probably keep in the freezer for as long as you can keep your hands off it. Wine, on the other hand, is a moving target. Vintages vary. And the wine undergoes constant and irreversible changes in the bottle: Rough textures soften. Color lightens. Fruit flavors wane. Other flavors emerge, which you might like better than the original fruit, or not.

Over time, if the fruit fades before the other flavors

come on, the wine can seem to lose its personality. This is a "dumb stage," an expression you might hear wine buffs bandying about. With Bordeaux and Cabernet Sauvignon, this often happens five to eight years after the vintage; with other wines, sooner.

Fortunately, wine changes gradually, and when things come into a happy balance, it lasts awhile. This is called a "drink window," and it's usually expressed in published tasting notes as something like "Drink 2001-2005." Whether you peg it yourself or rely on experts, a drink window should provide the information you need so you won't miss out on a wine at its best.

Does it get better with age?

Most wines taste a little rough when they're first bottled. As they age, they lose some or all of that roughness, some quickly, some over decades. Truth to tell, most wines taste best while they're young and fresh. Great wine develops and transforms itself in the bottle into something even better. Wines with track records for aging well represent a very small percentage of all the wine out there, even if you put it in terms of all the *good* wine out there. The tricky part is predicting which ones will improve with age to deliver unforgettable experiences. Top-class Bordeaux, Burgundy, Barolo, Port and Cabernet Sauvignon are among the wines that do gain extra layers of character and flavor after years in the cellar.

Too, not everyone likes those extra flavors and characteristics that wines develop with age. If you don't, why waste your money cellaring wine? Drink it when you like it.

The moment of truth: When the wine touches the lips

It is possible to get so wrapped up in the pursuit of wine, building wine cellars, memorizing vintages, discovering new wines and learning about the regions and the grapes, that we forget a simple truth: Everything revolves around those moments when we raise a glass of wine to inhale its fragrance and take a sip. The reason for learning about wine—the reason for this book—is to get the most out of those moments. Knowledge translates into buying savvy, which will help you find a wine that will deliver maximum pleasure for any given occasion. Tasting experience gives us a context for appreciating what's in that glass. Resources spent to build a cellar and age wine pay dividends when the wine is in optimum condition for drinking.

This may seem obvious, but it bears repeating. I know people who get so fascinated by the idea of wine that they forget its purpose is to deliver pleasure. Don't let that happen to you.

Some words on language

Let's face it, whatever your favorite subject, you can get so wrapped up in it that the way you talk about it sounds pretentious and silly. Ever listen to football commentators? It's the same with wine, except that our favorite drink carries extra baggage in the form of a long history of snobbism and elitism. James Thurber skewered the excesses of wine-speak brilliantly in a cartoon depicting a dinner party with the caption, "It's a naive domestic burgundy, but I think you will be amused by its presumption." Some years later another *New Yorker* cartoonist, William Hamilton, lampooned the opposite extreme when he drew a couple of yuppies discussing wine. About each wine mentioned by the first the other would say, "Dynamite wine."

Somewhere between these extremes lies a sane way to express what you want to say about wine. The biggest hurdle is that language is not particularly good at describing smells and tastes, except to relate them to something else that might be more familiar. Fortunately for wine drinkers, fermentation produces hundreds of aromatic and flavor chemicals that are often identical to those that occur elsewhere in nature, so when you smell cherries in a glass of Cabernet it might be because the same chemical that makes cherries smell like cherries is actually present.

Rest assured, it is not snobbish to say that a wine's smell or taste reminds you of whatever it reminds you of. Likewise, you can feel textures with your tongue that remind you of textiles you have felt with your hands. Wines will also remind you of other wines. Comparisons are fair game.

In this book, I try to use plain English and, wherever possible, relate the topic at hand to that moment when the wine touches the lips.

How much to know

There is no end to how much one can learn about wine. Some of it is really useful, hard-core information that helps narrow the choice of which wine to buy or which one to serve for dinner. Some of it falls under the heading of "cool stuff to know," which serves no purpose other than to help us understand and appreciate what went into making the wine.

Personally, I like to know cool stuff. I put a lot of it into this book. Feel free to ignore it.

How much to drink, how much to serve

Alcohol, which has salutary effects in moderation (see "Wine and Health," below), also limits how much a person can consume. For some, one glass is enough. For others, it's not a meal unless a full bottle has been consumed. Most of us stand somewhere in between. I, for example, know that I will be too mellow to get back to work or stay awake at the theater if I have more than two standard glasses of wine (of 4 to 5 ounces each) with a meal.

When I plan a multi-course dinner party, I generally allow one full bottle per person. I almost always have wine left over. Also, it's a good idea to front-load the wine menu. People tend to drink more early in the meal, so have an extra bottle of the apéritif and the first table wine ready. If my guests still have wine in their glasses after the main course, I just let them finish it with the cheese, but I always have an unopened bottle ready if necessary. I always pick a dessert wine, too, but about half the time it remains unopened. People often feel like they have had enough alcohol by then, particularly if they're driving home.

Shorter meals use less wine. Longer meals generally hew to that one-bottle limit, just spread among more wines. A rule of thumb is to allow one or two glasses per person per hour.

Wine and health

Moderate wine consumption has been shown to halve the risk of coronary heart disease, lower blood pressure and reduce some cancer risks. It's past the point where this is just a theory. Study after study comes up with the same results: moderate drinkers live longer and suffer fewer diseases of the heart and circulatory system than heavy drinkers or abstainers. For most adults, the benefits of moderate wine consumption overwhelm the risks. Research continues in an effort to learn just what it is about wine that produces such effects.

What is moderate consumption? The most conservative figures I've seen are one or two glasses per day. I've also seen recommendations as high as four or five glasses, which is more than a half bottle. (For the purposes of these calculations, a glass is four ounces.) Table wine of 12.5 percent alcohol provides about 100 calories per four-ounce glass.

Some things in wine can cause problems. Chief among

them is the alcohol itself. Alcoholics obviously must avoid wine. Anyone on medications that should not be combined with alcohol, or who have medical conditions compromised by alcohol, should also avoid wine. Diabetics must be aware of how much alcohol and sugar they might be consuming and monitor their intake accordingly.

Bottom line: For the most part, healthy humans can consume moderate amounts of wine guilt-free.

About sulfites

Some people—mostly severe asthmatics—are exquisitely sensitive to a family of chemicals called sulfites. One sulfite in particular, sulfur dioxide, is commonly used to clean winemaking equipment. It is added during the winemaking process to prevent spoilage. A tiny amount also occurs naturally in wine as a byproduct of fermentation. Those who are sensitive to sulfites usually know it, because sulfites occur in much higher concentrations in frozen shrimp and other foods. The federal government requires every bottle of wine to carry a label that says "contains sulfites." Modern winemaking techniques use other methods to retard spoilage, and thus minimize the addition of sulfites.

ABOUT "THE ESSENCE"

The love of wine, like any pursuit, can become as complicated or remain as simple as you like. Musicians study theory, harmony, and composition, but you can enjoy the symphonies of Beethoven or Tchaikovsky without knowing the first thing about key signatures or sonata form. A walk through the Louvre could satisfy your soul even if you can't tell Delacroix from Fragonard. It's the same with wine. What you know about it surely can enhance your appreciation, but it's not a prerequisite for enjoying the experience.

Even if you don't want to delve into the details, learning a few key concepts about wine can make drinking it that much more fun. That's why each chapter in this book begins with a brief summary, a distillation of the key messages within.

Rabbi Eleazar, a great medieval Jewish scholar, once was challenged by a member of his congregation to teach him the Talmud while standing on one leg. The Talmud, a dense and complex compilation of religious teachings, is a source of endless arguments for scholars. But Eleazar was up to the task. Balancing on one foot, he said, "Do unto others as you would have them do unto you. All the rest is commentary." If you listen in on serious wine enthusiasts, sometimes they can sound like Talmudic scholars, arguing over arcane topics. If I had to deliver it standing on one leg, my advice would be, "Drink what you like and keep trying new things." All the rest is commentary.

The Essence

Winemakers determine a wine's character and style by the decisions they make in the vineyard and the winery. Among the most critical vineyard decisions are the yield to aim for (generally, smaller crops make more flavorful wine) and when to pick the grapes (less ripe, ripe, or extra-ripe). In the winery, a whole series of choices at each step of the process can profoundly affect a wine's style.

Some wines depend on special techniques. Champagne, for example, requires a second fermentation to produce its characteristic bubbles. Dessert wines can get their sweetness by stopping fermentation before all the sugar is used up or by blending in unfermented grape juice or lightly fermented, heavily filtered wine.

Labels distinguish a particular wine from all others but often do not reveal matters of quality or style except through the reputation of the producer.

CHAPTER ONE

Why Wine Tastes Like It Does

At first glance, vineyards and wineries do pretty much the same thing everywhere grapes grow and are processed into wine. Yet each time we raise a new wine to our lips, we expect a different experience from the last one. The big reasons:

- Grape variety or varieties (i.e., Zinfandel tastes different from Pinot Noir)

- Location (i.e., Bordeaux delivers a slightly different experience from California Cabernet Sauvignon, even though they are largely made from the same grape)

- Style (i.e., the way Kendall-Jackson makes Cabernet as opposed to how Caymus does it)

Grape variety and geography are such critical factors that we use them for sorting out the vast wine world. A long wine list in a restaurant generally organizes its selections either by variety or by location. Within those categories, setting aside the matter of sheer excellence, what distinguishes one wine from another is style. Style is determined by how winemakers manage the growing cycle and the decisions they make in the winery.

This chapter describes in some detail how a grape grows and how it is made into wine. Ultimately, everything we savor in a glass of wine results from these processes. It helps to understand them before we explore grape varieties and geography.

Growing Season

Everything starts with the vine. It produces the grapes that make the wine, and it does what it does on an annual cycle. Dormant in winter, with the first warmth of spring it puts out tender buds that develop into shoots. In late spring, the shoots start to grow leaves and flowers. If all goes

IN THE SUMMER BB-SIZED GREEN GRAPES BEGIN TO APPEAR ON THE VINE. IF THE GROWER FINDS THAT THERE ARE TOO MANY OF THESE, HE WILL PRUNE A NUMBER OF BUNCHES TO LOWER THE YIELD.

well these flowers are pollinated and become tiny bunches of BB-sized green grapes. Each grape contains one or more seeds, which the vine makes to reproduce itself. Over the summer, these bunches mature and ripen, changing color from bright green to their mature hues, which can range from greenish yellow to purple to almost black. They also become very sweet; except for dates and a few exotics, grapes produce more sugar by far than other fruits. After harvest, the vine sheds its leaves and goes dormant for the winter, ready for the cycle to start again.

Each of these stages has a name, and if you hang around wine people you will probably hear references to them. They mark the key moments in the growing cycle. Recording the dates they occur provides a handy set of check points to differentiate one vintage from another.

- Bud break (early spring), when the vine comes to life after a winter of dormancy
- Flowering (late spring), when the first blossoms emerge
- Set (late spring, early summer) when the blossoms form tiny grape bunches
- Veraison (late summer, early fall), when the grapes start to lose their green color
- Maturity (fall), when the grapes produce enough sugar and flavor to be ready for picking

Viticulture

Left to its own devices, a grapevine will sprawl, spreading its tendrils far and wide. We know, from evidence dug up near Pompeii, that as long ago as Roman times grape growers figured out that planting the vines in rows and training the canes upward instead of outward would ripen more grapes and make them taste better. Vine-tending for the purpose of making wine is mentioned in the Bible.

The big decision for a vineyard is what variety to grow and, in regions that are susceptible to the root louse phylloxera, which of several resistant rootstocks to use. After that, viticulturists can manipulate several aspects of the vineyard, all of which make a difference. The space between the vines is critical. More vines per acre cost more to plant and tend, but allow each vine to produce less fruit, and usually that means better fruit. Also, more vines capture more of the sunlight falling on a particular vineyard, and pour more energy into the fruit. In cool regions, vines trained low to the ground absorb more heat reflected off the ground, which helps in their struggle to get ripe. In warmer regions, vines are trained higher so the grapes don't get too warm.

COOL-REGION VINES ARE TRAINED CLOSER TO THE GROUND.

Yield

Then there is the matter of yield, which is to say how much a given vineyard produces. In the New World grapes are measured in tons per acre, and are weighed as they reach the winery. In the Old World the measure is hectoliters per hectare, giving the actual volume of wine produced from a hectare (approximately 2.5 acres) of vineyard.

It's a little tricky converting from one to the other, because some varieties are juicier than others and some wineries press more liquid out of the grapes than others. Roughly, 14 hectoliters per hectare is equivalent to 1 ton per acre.

Yield is critical, probably the most important factor in wine quality after grape variety and vineyard site. Generally, the lower the yield the more intense the flavor in the resulting wine. Higher yields can produce weak wine. But this is not as straightforward as it sounds. There is a range of yields that make good wine, depending on the vineyard site and vine-training system. For example, conventional wisdom is that yields of three to four tons per acre are ideal for Cabernet Sauvignon, but vineyards producing as much as eight tons per acre have produced award-winning wine.

NARROWLY SPACED VINES COST MORE TO PLANT AND TEND, BUT ALSO YIELD LESS FRUIT PER VINE, WHICH MEANS BETTER FRUIT.

Growers can regulate yield by manipulating the grapevines at key stages. Pruning the vines in winter, they can choose how many canes to leave, and thus the number of bunches. In summer, after set, they can assess how generous Mother Nature has been and go through the vineyard to strip off some of the little green bunches. Europeans calls this "green harvest." Many modern growers prune for the largest yield that would still make good wine (so that they will have enough grapes even with a bad set); then, if the weather is too good, they can reduce the yield by stripping off the green bunches.

Harvest

It takes a vine longer to ripen a lot of grapes. Thus, low-yielding vineyards generally ripen earlier than those that are managed to produce more fruit. In some vintages, this can mean harvesting healthy grapes before a rainstorm that waterlogs the grapes still hanging in high-yielding vineyards. You can easily taste the difference in the wines.

As a grape ripens, physiological changes happen fast. A week or two before it's ripe a grape tastes virtually indistinguishable from a sour leaf. All that sweet flavor develops in the final few days. Sugar content shoots up, while acidity

HARVEST IS THE BUSIEST TIME IN THE VINEYARD.

AFTER HARVEST, THE GRAPES WILL BE CRUSHED AND READIED FOR FERMENTATION.

falls off. Flavor compounds develop like crazy. Ideally, the rest of the plant is going through physiological changes as well. Among the most important are those that soften the tannins in the stems, seeds and grape skins. (The tannins have the same chemistry as the component in tea leaves that makes overbrewed tea dry out your mouth.) As the stems turn from green to brown, the tannins change from mouth-puckeringly hard to sweet and velvety.

Ideally, all these changes occur before it's time to pick. In the real world, there's always weather. A storm is coming. A heat wave ripens the grapes faster than anticipated. A cold snap stops the ripening process. Rain or fog encourages mold and rot. This is when winemaking requires the steely nerves of a riverboat gambler.

Making wine

In perfect conditions, making wine is easy. Squish the grapes in a big vat and let the natural yeasts clinging to the skins go to work on the natural sugars, fermenting them into alcohol (which stays in the wine) and carbon dioxide (which dissipates). Press off the resulting wine, let it mature in barrels for a few months or a few years, and bottle it. But conditions are seldom perfect.

Winemakers manipulate the process to approximate the result of a perfect vintage. Each step can affect the character, the style and the quality of a wine. For example, natural yeasts sometimes fail to convert all the sugar into alcohol.

Winemakers can use cultured yeasts produced in a laboratory to ensure that fermentation goes smoothly and thoroughly. We know that cultured yeasts produce simpler flavors than the colonies of wild yeasts clinging to the grape skins, but we also want the wine to finish its fermentation to dryness.

Here, then, are some key winemaking decisions and the tools used to implement them in the winery:

Fermentation

Yeast is only one aspect of fermentation that requires a decision. Other biggies are how long to ferment and at what temperature. Fermentation produces heat. If you have ever baked bread, you know that the dough feels warmer after it has risen. The same type of fermentation occurs in wine. In general, warmer fermentation extracts more flavor, but the winemaker's goal is to find the balance between too much heat, which can make a wine taste cooked, and too little, which makes a fruity, simple wine.

Stainless steel vats wrapped with refrigeration jackets can control fermentation temperatures precisely. In European wine regions where it gets darned cold in October, they use small fermentation containers so that ambient air temperatures can keep the fermenting juice from getting too warm. In Burgundy, for example, white grapes are pressed first, then fermented in the same small oak barrels used for aging red wine (see Cellar Aging and Oak, below). In addition to preventing overheating, barrel fermentation adds extra layers of flavor to the finished wine. New World Chardonnay producers have largely adopted this same technique.

Doff your cap, please

Any solid matter in fermenting wine rises to the top, carried upward by carbon dioxide bubbles, forming a cap. In a large container, this can insulate the yeast cells from the oxygen they need to keep fermentation going. Winemakers use various methods to deal with this cap. One method is to push the cap back down into the wine periodically with a long-handled piece of wood. (A higher-tech version of this method uses a mechanical device to punch down the cap and runs the device around the winery from vat to vat on a rail system suspended from the ceiling.)

Many wineries simply pump the wine over the cap from the bottom. A modern invention, the rotary tank, solves the temperature and cap problems in one fell swoop by turning a refrigerated stainless steel tank on its side and allowing the winemaker to rotate the tank like a cement mixer. In Piedmont, some winemakers use a decidedly low-tech method that suspends a sort of lattice from the top of the vat, which prevents the cap from rising all the way to the top. Each of these methods affects the wine by extracting more or less tannin, and varying amounts of specific flavor components. Gentler methods generally produce softer wine.

Chaptalization

Used in cool wine regions or in poor years when grapes have a low natural sugar content, chaptalization is the addition of sugar to the grape juice or must before or during fermentation to produce enough alcohol or, in some cases, to extend fermentation to extract more flavor. The term honors Jean-Antoine Chaptal, Napoleon's minister of agriculture, who encouraged the practice. It is frequently used in Bordeaux and Burgundy in France, as well as Oregon and New York, although it is illegal in California and Italy.

Going to press

Putting a wine through a press separates the liquid from most of the solid matter. For red wines, the choice of when to press depends on how much color, flavor and tannin the winemaker wants to extract from the skins and seeds roiling around in the fermenting wine. Some choose to press early to make a softer wine. Others let the completely fermented wine remain in contact with the solid matter to make a more flavorful wine. The decision depends on the grape variety and where it was grown. Some varieties and sites take well to long maceration, and need the extra time to develop full flavor without making the wine too tough. Ultimately, it's a stylistic choice. Pressing happens before fermentation in white wines to extract less color and tannin.

The juice that will drain off by itself without pressing, called free run, is the prime stuff. Once the press starts squeezing, it extracts more tannin and other

PRESSING GRAPES SEPARATES ADDITIONAL JUICE FROM THE SKINS AND SEEDS.

materials that can roughen the texture. Winemakers usually divide this process into several portions, the results of which are called press fractions, each one progressively tougher and more tannic. Later, these fractions will be finished differently and may be blended back with the free run.

Malolactic fermentation

After the alcoholic (primary) fermentation, wine undergoes a secondary fermentation in which bacteria convert malic acid in grapes to lactic acid. Malic acid is the familiar tang in green apples. Lactic acid occurs in milk. Malolactic fermentation, thus, makes the wine taste softer, and adds some interesting aroma and flavor byproducts. This happens naturally when the wine gets warm enough.

Unfortunately, if it doesn't happen in the winery it can happen in the bottle. This would be bad, because byproducts of malolactic fermentation include fizzy texture and rank flavors (which disappear with exposure to air). To prevent this, many winemakers prefer to encourage the process by heating their cellars (or the temperature-

controlled tanks) after primary fermentation, or may even add commercial strains of malolactic bacteria to get the secondary fermentation done early.

In some wines, especially those in which the winemaker wants to preserve as much acidity as possible, malolactic fermentation is deliberately prevented. The old method was to add a lot of sulfur dioxide to the wine. Today, the preferred method is a sterile filtration to remove the malolactic bacteria.

Lees

Pressing only removes the big chunks from the wine. The fine sludge that settles to the bottom of a vat of pressed wine, called the lees, is a rich mixture of mostly dead yeast cells and other miscellaneous byproducts of fermentation mixed with teeny bits of grape. Leaving white wine in contact with lees while it ages in the cellar has a profound effect on the wine. It adds a distinctive, tangy flavor of its own, and encourages a smoother texture.

Racking

From time to time, winemakers transfer the wine from one container to another. This has several benefits. It exposes the wine to air, which can refresh it. It also affords an opportunity to separate the clear wine from the lees.

Selection

No two wines from two different fermentation vats or barrels taste exactly alike. They represent different vineyards, different parts of the vineyard, different stages of the harvest, different press fractions (see Going to Press, above). Even if the source material is identical, winemakers know that each fermentation container is a little different. Some barrels go bad. Inevitably, the result is a welter of similar but distinct wines.

The winemaker can throw it all together into one big vat before bottling, or make a careful selection. In some parts of the world and some wineries, it's as simple as tasting each lot and deciding, "This one is good enough, but this is not." Others take a more critical approach, sorting out the various lots according to style and making separate wines from them. They might, for example, collect all the best barrels into a "reserve" wine (the original meaning of the term before it was co-opted by medium-priced wineries trying to seem fancy), or more accurately, a "special selection."

Multiply this by all the different varieties a winery might make in Italy or California, and you can see why one vintner might joke that he makes hundreds of wines every year, even though he officially makes only five or six products.

REFRIGERATED STAINLESS STEEL TANKS CAN CONTROL FERMENTATION TEMPERATURES PRECISELY.

Blending

Any time a winemaker mixes together two or more lots, technically that's a blend. It can be as subtle as two lots of the same variety from the same vineyard, or as dramatic as different varieties grown in different regions. There is an art to it. Really good blenders can taste samples from dozens of vats and use one wine's acidity to offset another's flatness, or another wine's minty note to enhance yet another's ripe cherry flavor, with the result tasting better than any one of the bits by itself.

In some regions, it has become traditional to blend different grape varieties. In Bordeaux, for example, they can make red wine from Cabernet Sauvignon, Cabernet Franc, Merlot, Malbec and Petit Verdot in any combination. If a wine has a personality that asserts itself vintage after vintage, one reason could be a consistent blend.

Cellar aging and oak

Before there were stainless steel tanks, winemakers used whatever containers they had for holding the wine at various points in the process. The most common container was the hogshead, an oak barrel of about 60 gallons. It had several advantages, not least of which was that it could be

AGING WINE IN OAK BARRELS IMPARTS AN ESSENCE OF VANILLA, NUTMEG OR SMOKE.

moved about in the winery. Also, if one container went bad, it did not ruin the whole batch. In cool European cellars, a barrel prevented wine from getting too warm.

Holding wine in the winery before bottling, called cellar aging, mellows it and rounds out its texture. This can range from a short settling period for fresh white wines to extended aging in barrels for aristocratic reds. Oak barrels also impart flavors, primarily vanilla, maybe nutmeg, smoke or chocolate notes, sometimes the odor of freshly sawn wood. Because small barrels can affect the flavor of wine so directly, even adding extra tannin to the wine, winemakers who want to minimize this effect can use larger barrels, older barrels, or neutral containers such as glass-lined tanks or stainless steel.

To some, oak-aged wines taste like Jack Daniel's whiskey. A lot of wines are aged in oak but don't say so on the label. The ones that do say "oak-aged" on the label usually have a marked flavor imparted by barrels. But so do wines that may not reveal their oak sojourns. Tasting notes can help. If you don't like oak, avoid those that mention nutmeg or vanilla. You'll probably save yourself a lot of money; wines aged in oak tend to cost more.

Knowing that people like the sweet vanilla-smoky taste of oak in their wines, cost-conscious winemakers add oak chips, usually made by chopping up old barrels, to the unfinished wine. (It's the same principle as flavoring warm cider by soaking it with cinnamon sticks and cloves.) But the resulting flavors are more obvious than those that come from aging the wine in oak barrels.

About oak

There are three main species of oak that coopers employ in barrel making. *Quercus alba*, or American white oak, grows throughout North America, ranging from just south of the Canadian border across the eastern United States and parts of the Midwest through much of the southern United States, including Missouri and Arkansas. *Quercus sessiliflora*, or sessile oak, and *Quercus robur*, known variously as

English, French or Russian oak, range from the British Isles through France and Portugal, and extend east all the way into parts of Russia. Recently, coopers in Oregon have been using the state's local species, *Quercus garyanna*, to make barrels that impart a distinctive taste I liken to peaches.

There is no consensus on which species is best for cooperage, but in general barrels made from American oak are thought to impart stronger tannins and more vanilla and coconut flavors to the wine aged within them. Barrels made from European oak have a more subtle influence.

Only since the 1970s have American coopers concentrated on making barrels for wine rather than whiskey. American oak barrels are predominantly used for such strong reds as Australian Shiraz, Spanish Rioja and the warm-climate Cabernet Sauvignons and Zinfandels. The quality of the cooperage and seasoning of barrels can moderate the flavors imparted to a wine just as much as the species or origin of oak used.

As for European oak, France is the leading producer, thanks to excellent forestry practices. In winemaking, oak from the Nevers and Allier forests in France's two central regions is especially prized for quality, and can cost two to three times as much as its American counterpart.

Finishing wine: fining, filtering, spinning

These methods remove particles from wine. A fining agent (egg whites are traditional, but gelatins and other ingredients are also used) is introduced when a young wine is in the vat or barrel. As the agent settles through the wine, it collects various particles; when these fall to the bottom of the vat, the wine is carefully poured off and the particles remain behind.

Filtration is usually done just before bottling, to remove even smaller particles that might cloud the wine, or yeasts or sugars that might kick off a fermentation in the bottle. Some insist that these processes "strip" character from wines, but in my tasting of both filtered and unfiltered wine

I cannot say that these processes are always good or always bad. Careful winemakers on both sides of the issue make expressive wines.

Another way to remove fine particles is with a centrifuge, which runs the wine through a rapid spin cycle to separate the particles from the liquid. An even more high-tech device is the spinning cone, which can actually separate the alcohol and water from the wine solids.

Special techniques

Champagne

The classic method for making sparkling wine, used in the Champagne region of France, involves bottling a blend of still wines with an added mixture of sugar and yeast to induce a secondary alcoholic fermentation in the bottle. An important by-product of this fermentation is carbon dioxide, which dissolves into the wine and creates the fizz characteristic of sparkling wine.

The next step is to age the fermented wine in the bottle, allowing the wine to develop depth and flavor

DURING DISGORGING—AN ESSENTIAL STEP IN MAKING CHAMPAGNE—THE SEDIMENT (SHOWN HERE) IS REMOVED FROM THE NECK OF THE BOTTLE.

complexity from contact with the lees left after this bottle fermentation. Before finishing the wine, a process called riddling gently collects these dead yeast cells in the neck of the bottle. Traditionally, this involves shaking and turning the bottles by hand in a special rack to force the sediment into the neck. Today, in large wineries, giant machines rotate huge

A BARREL OF PORT—A SWEET WINE THAT IS FORTIFIED WITH BRANDY TO ELEVATE THE ALCOHOL LEVEL AND STOP THE FERMENTATION PROCESS.

crates of bottles at one time.

In a process called disgorging, the temporary crown caps (like the ones on old soda pop bottles) are removed, and the sediment is extracted by freezing the wine in the neck, which contains the sediment, and allowing the pressure in the bottle to blow it out. The bottles are then topped up with the *dosage*, a mixture of wine and sugar syrup which helps to offset naturally high acidity and creates a balanced sparkling wine. Then, the bottles are stoppered with the final cork and the wire muzzle is secured in place.

In a less labor-intensive method, the secondary fermentation occurs in a sealed vat, which also traps the carbon dioxide. The finished wine is bottled under pressure and does not require disgorging. This Charmat process is used for inexpensive sparkling wines and for wines that are made to emphasize their fruit flavors, such as Asti Spumante and Prosecco.

Sweet wines

So far, we have been focusing on dry (or, in some cases, nearly dry) table wines. Sweet wines use additional techniques to deal with two big questions: how to make the wine sweet, and how to keep it from fermenting again once it's bottled.

One way to make a wine sweet is to stop the fermentation before it consumes all the natural sugar in the grapes. Another method is to set aside a portion of barely fermented wine, and use this to sweeten the rest of the lot, which is fermented dry. To keep the fermentation from starting again, winemakers used to add a large dose of sulfur dioxide, but today the preferred technique is to microfilter the wine to remove any stray yeast cells that could induce another fermentation.

A high dose of alcohol also stops fermentation. This is the principle behind fortified wines, such as Port, in which the must—the unfermented grape juice—barely begins to ferment before brandy is added to lift the alcohol level beyond the point where yeast can survive.

To make very sweet wines requires very sweet grapes. In regions known for their sweet wines, moist conditions at harvest time produce a mold called *botrytis cinerea*. It attacks ripe grapes, dehydrating them and thus concentrating the sugar in them. This happens in the vineyards of Sauternes and Germany, creating the raw material for nectar that fetches the highest prices of any wine in the world.

If Mother Nature doesn't make the grapes sweet enough in the vineyard, several techniques can be deployed. In Northern Italy, bunches of grapes hang in warm attics for months until they dry into raisins. The wine made from this technique, called *passito*, has a raisiny flavor. (The same technique dessicates red grapes for a high-alcohol dry wine called Amarone.) Another technique involves freezing the grapes solid, then pressing them when they are partially thawed. Because syrup thaws at a lower temperature than water, the resulting juice is very sweet. Wines made with these techniques don't have the complexity of those made from botrytis-affected grapes, but they can be rich and seductive on their own merits.

Pushing the envelope: extreme styles

In various corners of the world, winemakers manipulate their wines into styles that are so unusual they create their own unique categories. In Australia, for example, they make a red sparkling wine from Shiraz. In Greece, pine barrels add a strong resiny character to *retsina*. In southern Spain, they make Sherry by exposing wine to severe oxidation and heat as it ages, even encouraging the growth of a special yeast (called *flor*). In central Italy, they seal up sweet juice in a barrel, literally cementing it shut, and leave it for several years in a warm place to make rich, sherry-like *vin santo*. In the French Alps, Jurançon winemakers intentionally oxidize their white wines to make a more delicate cousin to sherry, *vin jaune*.

Labels

These days, a wine label's primary function is to catch your eye on a crowded shelf. Legally, however, it must contain answers to several key questions.

1. **Who made it?** The producer's name is the most important piece of information on the label, because ultimately a wine's quality rests on the backs of those who labored to make it. Just as certain sports teams always seem to have winning seasons, certain wineries always seem to do better than their peers. The best also have a distinctive style. It pays to know which ones you like.

2. **What is it made from?** One way or another, the label tells you what grape variety was used to make the wine. In the New World the grape variety is usually plainly stated. In the Old World a geographical appellation does the same duty. They expect you to know that red Burgundy is made from Pinot Noir just as the makers of mayonnaise expect you to know that it's made from oil, eggs and lemon, simply because the law requires it.

3. **Where was it grown?** The geographical appellation tells you where it was grown. Appellations can be specific, down to a single vineyard, or general, encompassing a whole region or state.

4. **How is this lot different from the others?** Special designations can name a specific vineyard that produced the grapes for the wine, or identify the wine as a reserve bottling (which has a legal definition in the Old World—basically that a wine meets higher standards for ripeness or aging), as an estate bottling (which has a

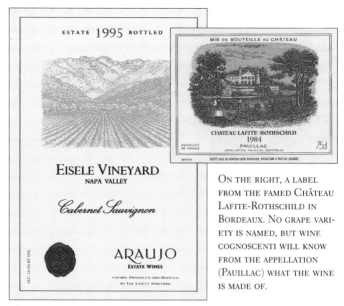

On the right, a label from the famed Château Lafite-Rothschild in Bordeaux. No grape variety is named, but wine cognoscenti will know from the appellation (Pauillac) what the wine is made of.

On the left, a label from Araujo Estate Wines in California. In addition to the producer's name, the grape variety (Cabernet Sauvignon) and a special designation (Eisele Vineyard) are prominently featured.

legal definition in the United States, basically that the winery owns or controls the vineyards that were used to make the wine) or as a special lot, as in the Australian practice of using bin numbers. (Historically, several of Australia's largest wineries labeled their wines with bin numbers instead of varietal names or proprietary names. Originally, this referred to the actual storage bin in which the wine was kept in the winery. Nowadays, it's just a fanciful name used for marketing purposes. Has a rough-and-tumble feel to it, doesn't it? Very Australian.)

5. **How old is it?** The vintage date tells you the year the grapes were harvested to make the wine. At the very least, it tells you how old the wine is (and remember that southern hemisphere harvests occur a half year earlier than those in the northern hemisphere, so a South African 1998 wine is about six months older than a 1998

from California). If you know anything about that vintage in that region, you also have a clue to what the wine might be like.

6. **The fine print.** U.S. labels require a number of details:

   a. An alcohol statement in percentage by volume. The law permits a 1.5% variance, so a wine labeled 12% alcohol could have as little as 10.5% or as much as 13.5%. In practice, a label that gives the alcohol percentage with a decimal (such as 12.7%) implies a greater degree of accuracy. A label that cites a round number (such as 12%) has probably been printed for use over many vintages and is being intentionally vague.

   b. "Produced and bottled by" is a phrase that has some meaning, because it indicates that the winery named on the label crushed the grapes and made the wine, or at least most of it (see Fudge Factors, below). If the wine was fermented elsewhere, it will say "Cellared and bottled by." If the wine is a blend of both, it can say "Made and bottled by." Any other similar terms are meaningless.

   c. Legal advisory. U.S. labels must say "Contains sulfites" if virtually any sulfur dioxide was used in the winemaking process, which is true of virtually every wine. They also must carry one of six mandated warnings, such as "Consumption of alcoholic beverages impairs your ability to drive a car or operate machinery, and may cause health problems." In 1999, the regulations were amended to allow one of two health advisory statements as well, such as "To learn the health effects of wine consumption, send for the Federal Government's Dietary Guidelines for Americans; Center for Nutrition Policy and Promotion, USDA, 1120 20th Street, NW, Washington, D.C. 20036 or visit its Web site: http://www.usda.gov/cnpp/guide.htm."

7. **The back label**. Wineries use the back label to provide extra information about the wine, the winery, or whatever they darn well please, as long as it's truthful. Most back labels are exercises in public relations, giving a romanticized history of the winery. Many devote the space to technical information about the wine, such as harvest dates, fermentation figures, lab data, and aging regimes. Some contain taste descriptions and even recommendations of food to accompany the wine. Who knows? You might even concur.

A good back label gives you some context for the wine. A great back label does it with style, even with humor. It's something amusing to read while your dinner partner is elsewhere.

8. **Fudge factors**

   a. The producer's name and address. Big wineries can skirt this one by creating DBAs ("doing business as" names) so it's not as useful as it might seem.

   b. The percentages. Internationally, laws and regulations seldom require 100 percent of anything, whether it's a vintage, region or grape variety. That's because wineries need to top up barrels and want the flexibility to add a dollop of this or that to make the wine better (or, in less scrupulous wineries, to stretch it). Most minimums are 85 percent.

What labels don't tell you

Nothing requires a wine label to reveal such crucial information as grape yield, degree of oak influence, or other matters of style, all of which bear critically on whether you will like the wine. The label simply distinguishes the wine from all other wines. Think of it that way, and you won't be led astray.

The Essence

Grapes reflect the place where they grow, as do all fruits, and wines only amplify that distinction. Grapes provide the raw material for wine, but geography explains why wine from the same grape variety grown in different places will taste different.

Of the hundreds of grape varieties, only a relative few are responsible for making most of the best wines:

CHARDONNAY

Chardonnay, Sauvignon Blanc, Riesling, Cabernet Sauvignon, Merlot, Pinot Noir and Syrah. Certain other varieties make outstanding wines in specific regions.

Most of the world names wines after the grape variety used to make them. In Europe, where long practice has identified certain varieties with certain regions, many wines are labeled only with the geographic area where they were made.

CHAPTER TWO

Grapes and Geography

Just as a Georgia peach tastes different from one grown in Texas, grapes grown in France make wine with a different set of characteristics from those of the same grape variety grown in Italy. Even more specifically, grapes from a vineyard on one hillside produce a set of flavors and textures distinct from the same grapes on another nearby hill. In short, every good wine starts with grapes growing in the right location.

Georgia peaches have a certain cachet because we know from experience the deliriously intense, juicy experience of eating them. It's not that the growers in Georgia are necessarily better than growers in Texas or California, but when it comes to raising peaches, they have the huge advantage of Georgia's geography. They also know which varieties do well in Georgia soils. Where it gets complicated is that growers in California, North Carolina or Texas, when they find a good place for an orchard and do their jobs well, can make similarly delicious peaches so sweet that you don't mind the juices rolling down your sleeve, either.

It's the same with wine. (Not the juice-down-the-sleeve part, but the quality.) Growers in France have the advantage of France's geography, and they grow varieties that do well in their soil. But France no longer has a monopoly on good places to grow grapes and make wine. The rest of the world is catching up, and in some cases surpassing the motherlands in Europe.

Whole books have been written about regions, districts, even single vineyards, in serious attempts to explore the meaning of all this. Many general wine books are organized entirely by geography. I'll try to compact all of that into the next two chapters, but first let's address the amazing range of grape varieties and build a framework for understanding why a little knowledge of geography can help you home in on a wine to drink tonight.

Grapes: the flavor key

Ampelography, the scientific classification of grapes, recognizes hundreds of individual varieties. It's possible to make wine from any fruit or vegetable that contains sugar so it can ferment into alcohol, but fine wine needs *Vitis vinifera*, the general class of grapes grown for wine in Europe. Other general classes, such as the American native grapes *Vitis labrusca* and *Vitis rotundafolia*, make wine that most people find odd. Stick to vinifera.

Grapevines like very particular conditions. Vinifera vines, in particular, thrive only in a relatively narrow swath of mild climates that stretches around the middle of the temperate zones of the globe. In the northern hemisphere, that cuts through Europe and the United States and in the Southern Hemisphere through parts of Argentina, Chile, New Zealand, Australia and South Africa. Smart grapegrowing can stretch the boundaries but Mother Nature pretty much has the upper hand on this one.

Centuries ago, after centuries of experimentation, Cistercian monks worked out that Chardonnay made the best white wine and Pinot Noir made the best red in their Burgundy vineyards. As production became more commercial, the makers of Burgundy had no reason to tell their customers that their white wines were made from Chardonnay any more than the makers of pickles need to remind their users that they used cucumbers. Anyone who wanted to make a wine taste more or less like white Burgundy would use Chardonnay, just as anyone who wanted to make a classic pickle would use cucumbers.

It took a while for the truth about varietals to sink in, but now most of the world identifies its wines by grape variety. In the Old World, the best wines don't mention grape names on the labels. France, Italy and Spain, for example, mostly use a geographic system to identify their wines, precisely because they have had several hundred years to figure out which grape varieties do best in which regions.

The exceptions within those countries are those regions in which the same winery makes individual wines from several different varieties. These regions include Alsace in France and most of northeastern Italy. They identify their wines by varietal.

CABERNET SAUVIGNON

(A third way to identify a wine on the label, proprietary names, frees the winemakers from occasional legal restrictions, allowing them to use whatever grapes they want in pursuit of better—or at least more marketable—wine. Proprietary labeling also clutters the landscape with a welter of names. Helpfully, most proprietary wines have back labels that describe the contents in detail.)

The widely grown grapes

Of the hundreds of grape varieties, a relative few have emerged as the ones responsible for making better wines in several places around the world. They each make wine with specific characteristics, summarized briefly in the following list.

White

Chardonnay Characteristics range from citrus and green apple in cool climates to pear, tropical fruit and fig in warmer areas, almost always complicated with some spice, vanilla and toasty notes from contact with oak.

Sauvignon Blanc Cool climates make wine tasting of citrus or passion fruit, and—as the flavors become progressively more extreme—herbs, olives, celery and green peppers. Riper grapes produce flavors of apple and fig.

41

Wines tend to be leaner than Chardonnay, except for those fermented in barrel like Chardonnay.

Riesling Peach, citrus, mineral and floral characteristics on a relatively light frame, often with some sweetness from sugar. Very sweet wines can taste of exotic fruits and honey.

Red

Cabernet Sauvignon A high level of natural tannin requires longer aging than most reds, which complicates the flavor profile. Grape-specific characteristics center around fresh currant (cassis) and cherry notes, often with herb or even vegetal overtones.

Merlot Similar to Cabernet, often less alcoholic and therefore faster-maturing.

Pinot Noir Texture and flavors tend to be less dense than Cabernet and center more around berry and, when really ripe, plum flavors. It has the ability to reflect small changes in growing conditions more deeply than most grapes, which begets wines of endless variety.

Syrah Bigger, more muscular than Pinot Noir. Flavors tend toward berry, plum and anise (often cited as licorice or black pepper), the best suggesting other exotic spices as well.

JOHANNISBERG RIESLING

Grapes identified with certain regions

These can make outstanding wines in certain places that have adopted them as their hallmarks, though they sporadically do well elsewhere as well.

White

Chenin Blanc Reaches its apex in the Loire, where it makes soft, pretty, lightly sweet Vouvray—which tastes of green apple—plus some amazingly rich and complex dessert wines and a few steely-dry wines that age well.

Gewürztraminer With its distinctive floral, peppery, spicy aromas, rich texture and slightly bitter flavors often suggesting grapefruit, this grape thrives best in Alsace (France).

Muscat Of dozens of Muscat varieties, most share a light texture, delicious fruit flavors suggesting litchi and tropical fruits, and spicy overtones. Does best in Piedmont (Northern Italy), where it makes the refined, lightly sparkling dessert wine Moscato d'Asti and the sweeter, more carbonated Asti Spumante.

Pinot Blanc A long-ago mutation of Pinot Noir, it makes soft, round white wines with apple and floral flavors. Best in Alsace and, as Pinot Bianco, Northeastern Italy.

Pinot Gris Another mutation of Pinot Noir, it often shows distinct melon flavors. Most familiar, though not often outstanding, as Italy's Pinot Grigio. Better in Alsace and Oregon.

Sémillon Bordeaux grows it to blend with Sauvignon Blanc for white wines, adding rounder texture and flavors reminiscent of fig and hay. Hunter Valley (Australia) makes it into a tight white wine that develops in 8-10 years into round, rich wines with distinctive lanolin notes.

Traminer Without the "gewürz" prefix. A lighter relative, with similar but less distinct flavors, although some regions use the names interchangeably.

Viognier Ripens well, making alcoholic wines with exotic, floral flavors that remind me of hopped-up Riesling. Condrieu (France) is the homeland, but it's becoming more important in California.

Red

Barbera Best in Piedmont (Northern Italy), where its racy acidity and berry flavors go well with the rich local cuisine and can age for years.

Dolcetto Best in Piedmont (Northern Italy), where its light texture and pretty berry flavors make it ideal for drinking young.

Gamay The grape of Beaujolais (France), tasting of berries with floral overtones; best consumed young.

Grenache One of the world's most widely planted grapes makes soft, round wines with flavors of berry and red cherry. In southern Rhône (France) it is the prime component of Châteauneuf-du-Pape.

Nebbiolo The grape of Barolo and Barbaresco (Piedmont, Northern Italy) has flavors of berry, cherry, a distinctive overtone of tar and, sometimes, rose petals. Tannic versions can require years of aging to soften.

Sangiovese The prime red grape of Tuscany makes everything from light everyday styles of Chianti with simple berry flavors to more ageable and distinguished wines in specific areas of Tuscany.

Tempranillo Most important in Spain, where it is the prime component of Rioja and other reds. Prized for its lithe texture and generous berry and cherry flavors.

Zinfandel At its best makes ripe, generous wines with berry, cherry, plum and spice flavors in California. Same as Primitivo in Southern Italy, where it makes similar, heady wines.

Some oddballs

From time to time, you might encounter interesting wines made from some of the following grapes and identified as such on a bottle.

White

Chasselas An important grape in Switzerland, where its natural softness retains enough acidity to make a balanced white wine.

Tocai In Northeastern Italy it makes light, fragrant dry white wines often called Tocai Friulano, not to be confused with—

Tokaji Not a grape variety but a Hungarian wine based on the grape Furmint, which can make rich, delicious dessert wines, not to be confused with—

Tokay No longer permitted in Alsace as a synonym for Pinot Gris, but still used in Australia for Liqueur Tokay, a dessert wine made from Muscadelle and aged for decades into marvelously spicy nectar. (Got all that?)

Verdelho The workhorse grape for anonymous white wines in Portugal and Australia.

Pinot Noir

Red

Cabernet Franc A Bordeaux blending grape, it stars on its own in a few Bordeaux wines (most notably Château Cheval Blanc) and in Anjou and Touraine (France). Lighter and less tannic than Cabernet Sauvignon, it often has stronger herbal flavors.

Malbec Another Bordeaux blending grape, it's found a home in Argentina, where its soft texture and pretty berry flavors make it the star.

Primitivo See Zinfandel, above

Clones

Grapevines are propagated not from seed but from cuttings taken from last year's growth. For centuries growers have carefully selected cuttings from vines with certain characteristics. Inevitably, some vines will produce more succulent fruit than others, or tighter clusters, or looser clusters, or leafier vines, or less leafy vines, and dozens of other traits. Ultimately, these selections result in distinct clones, each clone with a set of characteristics different from the others.

Nowadays, vine nurseries propagate specific clones and identify them for sale to growers.

You can see the difference from one clone to another in the vineyard, but what really counts is when you can taste the difference in the wines they make. Some differences are dramatic. The clones of Pinot Noir grown in Champagne yield bigger bunches with less color than the clones grown in Burgundy. Whether that's a natural adaptation to a cooler climate or careful selection and propagation by growers, the result is ideal for Champagne. The wines pick up less color.

Most Burgundy growers make it a point to have several clones in their small plots of vineyard as a means of creating more complexity in the finished wines. In theory, each clone makes wine with slightly different character and the mix is more interesting than any one clone by itself. Nebbiolo growers in Italy do the same. In Tuscany,

Brunello of Montalcino and Prugnolo of Montepulciano have turned out to be regional clones of Sangiovese.

The regions: the character key

Every region that makes wine eventually becomes associated with specific grape varieties. Certain growers often can do well with other wines, and sometimes they must overcome restrictive rules to show that they can. But even the newer winegrowing regions quickly establish reputations for certain kinds of wine.

Certain grapes do best in certain places because of the geography of the vineyard, primarily its climate but also the geology of the soil and the tilt and aspect of the slope. It's why the same grape grown in this vineyard over here in the same way by the same grower makes a different wine than another vineyard over there. The French have a word for it: *terroir*. (For a more thorough discussion of *terroir*, see chapter 5.)

The next two chapters summarize in very broad strokes the geography, the viticulture and the wines produced in the main wine regions of the world.

MERLOT

The Essence

This chapter outlines the key regions for fine wine in France, Italy, Spain, Portugal and Germany, explaining the geography, defining the grape varieties used in each area and describing the wines each one makes.

CHÂTEAU LAFITE ROTHSCHILD, BORDEAUX.

CHAPTER THREE

The Old World

France

Other countries produce more, but France defined fine wine. For the past half century or more, most of the world has either copied or tried to improve upon what France does with wine, often producing worthy alternatives. Many of the best French producers have responded to the challenge from other countries by improving their wines, to the point where France clearly makes more excellent wine today than ever before.

Bordeaux

Bordeaux is France's most thoroughly organized region. Many of the top wines are catalogued into quality levels. The most famous example, the 1855 Médoc Classification (see page 52), identified about five dozen châteaus in St. Estèphe, St. Julien, Margaux and Pauillac and one in Graves, sorting them into five levels of quality—called in English first growth, second growth, etc.—based largely on their selling prices at the time. Nearly a century and a half later, it remains remarkably accurate, although some wines have proved to be consistently better than others of the same rank. Other districts in Bordeaux have followed suit with their own classifications (see pages 53, 54).

This works for Bordeaux because the properties tend to be contiguous chunks of vineyard (although the law permits any château to bottle its wine from all of its land in the named district). Each château puts its name on one red wine blend and sometimes a white wine blend. Contrast that to other regions, where one producer may make wines from several different vineyards in several different subregions.

(Many châteaus bottle as a second wine those lots that don't make the final blend. Château Lafite-Rothschild, for example, also makes Carruades de Château Lafite. In good

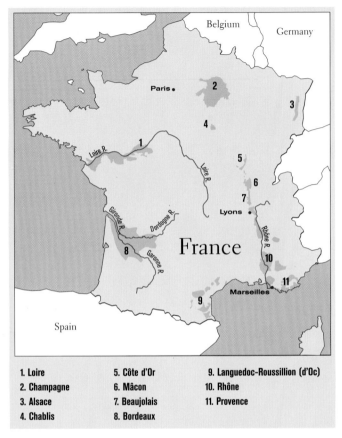

1. Loire
2. Champagne
3. Alsace
4. Chablis
5. Côte d'Or
6. Mâcon
7. Beaujolais
8. Bordeaux
9. Languedoc-Roussillion (d'Oc)
10. Rhône
11. Provence

vintages, these second wines can be far better than the first wines of many lesser châteaus. See page 56 for a list.)

BORDEAUX RED

Geography: The region is huge, and mostly flat; its greatest vineyards are on barely sloping ground near the Gironde estuary. St-Émilion is a hill surrounded by flat vineyards. Pomerol is a small rise in the midst of flatness. In both cases, most of the best vineyards are on the rises.

Grapes: Cabernet Sauvignon, Cabernet Franc, Merlot, Malbec, Petit Verdot.

Key wines: Médoc (including **St.-Estèphe, St.-Julien,**

Margaux and **Pauillac**) and Graves (mostly **Pessac-Léognan**) rely primarily on Cabernet. **St.-Émilion** and **Pomerol**, on the opposite side of the Gironde, rely on Merlot, though all five varieties grow in all regions. Some lesser wines are identified by grape variety.

Unique in the world, the top red wines of Bordeaux are made in enough quantity to be widely available. Many of the well-known châteaus make 25,000 cases a year, roughly 10 to 20 times what a typical Burgundian vintner can produce. This, coupled with Bordeaux's ageability in good vintages, means that the older wines you are most likely to encounter are Bordeaux. Most châteaus grow a mix of grape varieties, some that ripen early and some that ripen late, to ensure that they can make some wine even in poor harvest conditions. Each château thus has developed its own distinctive blend.

The region also makes oceans of commodity wine, simple reds meant for ready consumption. These wines tend to be lighter and less distinctive, though they can represent very good value. Many carry regional names, rather than individual château names, but it's perfectly legal to bottle these wines under the name of a fictitious château, as long as they make no claims to quality with such terms as *cru classé*. Though hundreds of legitimate small châteaus do make good to very good wine, Bordeaux can be a minefield of unfamiliar names. Rely on recommendations, and ultimately your own preferences.

BORDEAUX WHITE

Geography: Graves, where the region's the best dry whites come from, is mostly flat, similar to the Médoc. Soils tend to be gravelly, and therefore extremely well drained. Vineyards close to the water develop fog and mists around harvest time, which encourages the growth of *botrytis cinerea*, a mold that, rather than ruining the grapes, leads to luscious sweet wines.

Grapes: Sauvignon Blanc and Sémillon primarily, with

THE BORDEAUX CLASSIFICATIONS

THE 1855 OFFICIAL CLASSIFICATION OF THE MÉDOC

First Growths
Premiers Crus

Lafite-Rothschild (Pauillac)
Margaux (Margaux)
Latour (Pauillac)
Haut-Brion (Graves)
Mouton-Rothschild (Pauillac)

Second Growths
Deuxièmes Crus

Rauzan-Ségla (Margaux)
Rauzan-Gassies (Margaux)
Léoville-Las Cases (Saint-Julien)
Léoville-Poyferré (Saint-Julien)
Léoville-Barton (Saint-Julien)
Durfort-Vivens (Margaux)
Gruaud-Larose (Saint-Julien)
Lascombes (Margaux)
Brane-Cantenac (Margaux)
Pichon-Longueville-
   Baron (Pauillac)
Pichon-Longueville, Comtesse de
   Lalande (Pauillac)
Ducru-Beaucaillou (Saint-Julien)
Cos d'Estournel (Saint-Estèphe)
Montrose (Saint-Estèphe)

Third Growths
Troisièmes Crus

Kirwan (Margaux)
d'Issan (Margaux)
Lagrange (Saint-Julien)
Langoa-Barton (Saint-Julien)
Giscours (Margaux)
Malescot Saint-Exupéry (Margaux)
Boyd-Cantenac (Margaux)
Cantenac-Brown (Margaux)
Palmer (Margaux)
La Lagune (Haut-Médoc)

Desmirail (Margaux)
Calon-Ségur (Saint-Estèphe)
Ferrière (Margaux)
Marquis d'Alesme-Becker (Margaux)

Fourth Growths
Quatrièmes Crus

Saint-Pierre (Saint-Julien)
Talbot (Saint-Julien)
Branaire-Ducru (Saint-Julien)
Duhart-Milon-Rothschild (Pauillac)
Pouget Cantenac (Margaux)
La Tour-Carnet (Haut Médoc)
Lafon-Rochet (Saint-Estèphe)
Beychevelle (Saint-Julien)
Prieuré-Lichine (Margaux)
Marquis-de-Terme (Margaux)

Fifth Growths
Cinquièmes Crus

Pontet-Canet (Pauillac)
Batailley (Pauillac)
Haut-Batailley (Pauillac)
Grand-Puy-Lacoste (Pauillac)
Grand-Puy-Ducasse (Pauillac)
Lynch-Bages (Pauillac)
Lynch-Moussas (Pauillac)
Dauzac (Margaux)
d'Armailhaq (Pauillac) (previously
   Château Mouton-Baronne-
   Philippe)
du Tertre (Margaux)
Haut-Bages-Libéral (Pauillac)
Pédesclaux (Pauillac)
Belgrave (Haut-Médoc)
de Camensac (Haut-Médoc)
Cos-Labory (Saint-Estèphe)
Clerc-Milon (Pauillac)
Croizet-Bages (Pauillac)
Cantemerle (Haut-Médoc)

THE 1855 OFFICIAL CLASSIFICATION OF SAUTERNES–BARSAC

First Great Growth
Premier Cru Supérieur

d'Yquem

First Growths
Premiers Crus

La Tour-Blanche
Lafaurie-Peyraguey
Clos Haut-Peyraguey
de Rayne-Vigneau
Suduiraut
Coutet
Climens
Guiraud
Rieussec
Rabaud-Promis
Sigalas-Rabaud

Second Growths
Deuxièmes Crus

de Myrat
Doisy-Daëne
Doisy-Dubroca
Doisy-Védrines
d'Arche
Filhot
Broustet
Nairac
Caillou
Suau
de Malle
Romer-du-Hayot
Lamothe-Despujols
Lamothe-Guignard

THE 1959 OFFICIAL CLASSIFICATION OF THE GRAVES

Other than Haut-Brion, the 1855 classifications did not include the châteaus of Graves; the best were classified separately in 1959 into an unranked list divided into red and white wines. In 1987, the subappellation Pessac-Léognan was created, dividing Graves roughly in two. All the classified estates fall within this new appellation, but they may legally use either Graves or Pessac-Léognan on their labels.

Classified Red Wines of Graves/Pessac-Léognan

Bouscaut
Haut-Bailly
Carbonnieux
Domaine de Chevalier
de Fieuzal
d'Olivier
Malartic-Lagravière
La Tour-Martillac
Smith-Haut-Lafitte
Haut-Brion
La Mission-Haut-Brion
Pape-Clément
Latour-Haut-Brion

Classified White Wines of Graves/Pessac-Léognan

Bouscaut
Carbonnieux
Domaine de Chevalier (Léognan)
d'Olivier (Léognan)
Malartic Lagravière (Léognan)
La Tour-Martillac (Martillac)
Laville-Haut-Brion (Talence)
Couhins-Lurton (Villenave d'Ornan)
Couhins (Villenave d'Ornan)
Haut-Brion (Pessac) (added in 1960)

THE 1985 OFFICIAL CLASSIFICATION OF ST-ÉMILION

The St-Émilion Wine Growers' Union first drew up a Classification in 1955. It has been revised twice, most recently in 1985. A new revision is underway now and should be published soon.

First Growths
Premiers Crus Classés — A

Ausone
Cheval Blanc

First Growths
Premiers Crus Classés — B

Beauséjour-Duffau La Garrosse
Belair
Canon
Clos Fourtet
Figeac
La Gaffeliére
Magdelaine
Pavie
Trottevieille

Grands Crus Classés

L'Angelus
L'Arrosée
Balestard La Tonnelle
Beausejour-Becot
Bellevue
Bergat
Berliquet
Cadet Piola
Canon-La-Gaffeliére
Cap de Mourlin
Le Chatelet
Chauvin
Clos Des Jacobins
Clos La Madeleine
Château Clos de l'Oratoire
Clos Saint-Martin
La Clotte
La Clusiére
Corbin
Corbin Michotte
Couvent Des Jacobins
Croque-Michotte

---

occasional small doses of spicy Muscadelle, tart Ugni Blanc and fruity Colombard.

Key wines: Pessac-Léognan, Graves (dry); Sauternes, Barsac, Cadillac, Loupiac (sweet).

The hilly Entre-Deux-Mers area makes oceans of ho-hum white wine, but the sweet wines and a few of the dry whites in Pessac-Léognan can be astounding. The better dry wines are often barrel-fermented to become spicy and rich, but many are simple, refreshing expressions of the grassy, tobacco-scented aspects of the primary grapes.

The sweet wines, especially Sauternes and Barsac, have glorious intensity and richness and rank among the great dessert wines.

Curé-Bon-La-Madeleine	Pavie-Decesse
Dassault	Pavie-Macquin
La Dominique	Pavillon-Cadet
Faurie de Souchard	Petit-Faurie-de-Soutard
Fonplégade	Le Prieuré
Fonroque	Ripeau
Franc-Mayne	Saint-Georges-Coat-Pavie
Grand-Barrail-Lamarzelle-Figeac	Sansonnet
Grand-Corbin	La Serre
Grand-Corbin Despagne	Soutard
Grand-Mayne	Tertre-Daugay
Grand-Pontet	La Tour-du-Pin-Figeac
Gaudet-Saint-Julien	(Giraud-Belivier)
Haut-Corbin	La Tour-du-Pin-Figeac (Moueix)
Haut-Sarpe	La Tour-Figeac
Lanoite	Trimoulet
Larcis-Ducasse	Troplong-Mondot
Lamarzelle	Villemaurine
Larmande	Yon-Figeac
Laroze	
Matras	
Mauvezin	
Moulin-du-Cadet	
L'Oratoire	

Burgundy

Burgundy adds a few more layers of complication to the Bordeaux model. Imagine if Château Lafite-Rothschild were divided up among 20 or 30 different owners, each of which could make its own wine called Lafite. That's the case in Burgundy, where dozens of different owners each have a few rows of vines in vineyards such as Bâtard-Montrachet, one of the most celebrated for white wine. The same situation repeats throughout the region. Each of these owners may also have portions of other scattered vineyards.

There is also a hierarchy of vineyard designations within each district or commune. At the bottom is **Bourgogne**, the regional designation, made from grapes grown anywhere in Burgundy. Next step up are wines named after **subregions**,

The Important Second Labels of Bordeaux

Second Label (Appellation)	Estate
Abeille de Fieuzal (Pessac-Léognan)	Château de Fieuzal
Blason d'Issan (Margaux)	Château d'Issan
Carruades de Lafite Rothschild (Pauillac)	Château Lafite Rothschild
Château Canuet (Margaux)	Château Cantenac-Brown
Château Haut-Bages-Avérous (Pauillac)	Château Lynch-Bages
Château Labat (Haut-Médoc)	Château Caronne-Ste.-Gemme
Château Moulin Riche (St.-Julien)	Château Léoville Poyferré
Domaine de Larrivet (Pessac-Léognan)	Château Larrivet-Haut-Brion
Frank Phélan (St.-Estèphe)	Château Phélan-Ségur
La Bastide de Siran (St.-Estèphe)	Château Cos-Labory
La Dame de Montrose (St.-Estèphe)	Château Montrose
La Parde de Haut-Bailly (Pessac-Léognan)	Château Haut-Bailly

such as Chablis, Mâcon, Côtes de Nuits. Next come wines named after the closest **Village**, such as Volnay or Nuits-St-Georges. **Premier cru** is next, attaching the vineyard name and the name of the nearest village, such as Volnay-Champans. **Grand cru** is the top designation, carrying only the vineyard name and, helpfully, the words "*grand cru.*"

Prices increase with the finer distinctions. Quality often follows, but not always. Better producers who make superior wines across their entire range can often make simple village wines that taste much better than lesser producers' best *grands crus*. The best approach to Burgundy is to identify those producers whose styles you like best and focus on their wines.

Geography: In Chablis, the vineyards cluster on hills that face the Yonne River. The vineyards in the Côte de Nuits and Côte de Beaune (collectively called the Côte d'Or) stretch along the eastern slopes of the Massif Central, the mountainous region that dominates central France, right

Second Label (Appellation)	Estate
La Réserve de Léoville Barton (St.-Julien)	Château Léoville Barton
La Sirène de Giscours (Margaux)	Château Giscours
Les Charmes de Kirwan (Margaux)	Château Kirwan
Les Fiefs de Lagrange (St.-Julien)	Château Lagrange
Les Forts de Latour (Pauillac)	Château Latour
Les Hauts de Smith (Pessac-Léognan)	Château Smith-Haut-Lafitte
Les Pagodes de Cos (St.-Estèphe)	Château Cos-d'Estournal
Mondot (St.-Emilion)	Château Troplong-Mondot
Pavillon Rouge du Château Margaux (Margaux)	Château Margaux
Pensées de Lafleur (Pomerol)	Château Lafleur
Réserve de la Comtesse (Pauillac)	Château Pichon-Longueville-Lalande
Sarget de Gruaud-Larose (St.-Julien)	Château Gruaud-Larose
Ségla (Margaux)	Château Rauzan-Ségla
Tourelles de Longueville (Pauillac)	Château Pichon-Longueville-Baron

where the slopes end and the flat plains begin. The best vineyards in each region are mid-slope and face southwards to catch the most warmth and sunlight in what are cool-weather latitudes.

Grapes: Exclusively Chardonnay for white and Pinot Noir for red in the better vineyards. In lesser regions, Pinot Blanc and Aligoté are permitted for white, Gamay for red.

Key wines: Bourgogne Blanc, Bourgogne Rouge, Chablis (all white), Côte de Nuits (almost entirely red), Côte de Beaune (red and white), Côte Chalonnaise (mostly white, but some red), Mâcon (mostly white) and Beaujolais (mostly red). (See *Grands crus*, page 58.)

Key producers: In Burgundy, domaines bottle wine from their own grapes and négociants buy grapes or wine from independent growers. Some négociants also have their own domaines. Hundreds of small domaines make some of the greatest Burgundies in very small quantities. Their

GRAND CRU APPELLATIONS OF BURGUNDY

Bienvenues-Bâtard-Montrachet	Criots-Bâtard-Montrachet
Bonnes-Mares	Echezeaux
Bâtard-Montrachet	Grands Echezeaux
Chablis Grand Cru	Griotte-Chambertin
Chambertin	La Grande Rue
Chambertin-Clos de Bèze	La Romanée
Chapelle-Chambertin	La Tâche
Charlemagne	Latricières-Chambertin
Charmes-Chambertin	Mazis-Chambertin
Chevalier-Montrachet	Mazoyères-Chambertin
Clos de La Roche	Montrachet
Clos de Tart	Musigny
Clos de Vougeot	Richebourg
Clos des Lambrays	Romanée-Conti
Clos Saint-Denis	Romanée-Saint-Vivant
Corton	Ruchottes-Chambertin
Corton-Charlemagne	

wines are very hard to find. Some large, high-quality négociants whose wines are widely distributed are Jadot, Drouhin, Faiveley, Bouchard, Duboeuf, Leroy, O. Leflaive and Verget.

SOME RED BURGUNDIES

- **Chambolle-Musigny**, in the middle of the Côte de Nuits, has a lot of limestone in its soils and the wines tend to be among the most delicate in Burgundy.

- **Musigny**, mid-slope and immediately south of Chambolle's boundary, is much richer, but still among the most delicate of *grand cru* red Burgundies.

- **Vosne-Romanée's** vineyards are fanned out on a vaguely amphitheater-like slope behind the village. The wines combine richness with elegance at every quality level.

- **Richebourg**, the highest up the slope of all of Vosne-Romanée's seven *grands crus* (the most in Burgundy), makes bold, densely textured reds.

THE HILLS NEAR MAISON LOUIS LATOUR IN THE CÔTE D'OR, BURGUNDY.

- **Volnay** covers a hillside in the middle of the Côte de Beaune and consistently makes remarkably refined reds, but no *grands crus*.

- **Pommard**, next door to Volnay, has more clay in its soil and the wines are totally different—muscular and firm-textured. It also has no *grands crus*.

SOME WHITE BURGUNDIES

- **Chablis**, northernmost and coolest, with its chalky soils replete with tiny fish fossils, makes steely, tart white wines.

- **Meursault**, Puligny-Montrachet and Chassagne-Montrachet, clustered around the scrubby little hill of Montrachet (literally "bald mountain") in the Côte de Beaune, make rich, creamy, dry white wines.

- **Mâcon**, which includes Pouilly-Fuissé, makes easy-drinking, generous, open-textured wines in low rolling hills in the warmer, southern part of Burgundy.

Champagne

Champagne gets fizzy by undergoing a second fermentation in the bottle. (See page 31 for details.)

Geography: Champagne is the northernmost wine region in France, and therefore the coolest. Its chalky soils and gently rolling hills can barely ripen the grapes. Naturally high acidity and low sugar in the grapes come into balance after the secondary fermentation.

Grapes: Chardonnay, Pinot Noir, Pinot Meunier.

Key wines: By sugar level, from driest to sweetest: Brut, Extra Dry, Demi-Sec, Sec, Doux. (Note that even Extra Dry is slightly sweet). By style: Blanc de Blancs is made entirely from Chardonnay, Blanc de Noirs entirely from Pinot Noir and Pinot Meunier. Non-vintage Champagne is blended from several vintages to make a consistent product in a consistent style.

Although the public never sees it, Champagne uses an internal classification system for its vineyards, with the top vineyards rated 100 percent, others lower. By juggling such elements as the vineyard sources, grape varieties and aging regimens, each winery develops its own distinct style. Even when Pinot Noir and Pinot Meunier make up the majority of the blend, most Champagne has little to no red color because the grapes are lightly pressed and the clear juice drawn off before primary fermentation.

Key producers: Billecart-Salmon, Bollinger, Deutz, Charles Heidsieck, Piper Heidsieck, Jacquesson, Krug, Lanson, Laurent-Perrier, Perrier-Jouët, Pol Roger, Louis Roederer, Ruinart, Taittinger, Veuve-Clicquot.

Loire

Geography: From the Atlantic coast, the Loire River extends 600 miles inland through some of the greenest, prettiest wine country in the world. Castles line the lower half of the river. As one moves inland, the weather gets progressively warmer. The Melon grape grown near the town of Nantes on the coast produces the simple, charming white wine known as Muscadet. Neighboring Anjou grows Cabernet Franc and even some Gamay for rosé and light reds, plus a little Chenin Blanc primarily for sparkling wine.

Chinon grows Cabernet Franc for agreeable red wines. Vouvray, near Tours, grows Chenin Blanc for off-dry wines and, in favorable vintages, noble sweet wines. Finally, 250 miles inland, we come to Sancerre and Pouilly (whose best wine is Pouilly-Fumé), across the river from one another; it is warm enough here to ripen Sauvignon Blanc for white wine and in Sancerre some Pinot Noir for red.

Grapes: Melon, Chenin Blanc and Sauvignon Blanc for white, Pinot Noir, Cabernet Franc and Cabernet Sauvignon for red.

Key wines: Muscadet, Vouvray, Sancerre and Pouilly-Fumé (whites); Chinon, Sancerre (reds); Anjou (rosé).

Key producers: B. Baudry, Henri Bourgeois, Lucien Crochet, de Ladoucette, D. Dageneau, Fouquet, Huët, Joguet, Luneau-Papin, Metairau.

Alsace

Geography: Vineyards range along the foothills of the Vosge, not far from where the Rhine River defines the border between France and Germany. The cool northern climate is only suitable for white wine. In recent years Alsace has identified a roster of specific vineyards as *grands crus*, which wineries can identify as such on their labels. Most do, because the wines are most distinctive and bring higher prices.

Grapes: Riesling, Pinot Blanc, Pinot Gris, Gewürztraminer, Muscat.

Key wines: Varietally labeled (except for Edelzwicker, a blend). Dry wines tend to be ripe and taste distinctly of the aromatic grapes from which they are made. **Vendange Tardive** (late harvest) wines are higher in alcohol, sometimes sweet, and often very dramatic in style. **Sélection des Grains Nobles** (wines made from botrytis-affected grapes) can be as rich, sweet and seductive as any dessert wine in the world.

Key producers: Hugel, Josmeyer, Trimbach, Zind-Humbrecht.

Rhône

Geography: The Rhône River, which connects central France to the Mediterranean, rolls through craggy hills in the Northern Rhône region, then winds through rocky plains and low hills in the Southern Rhône.

Grapes: Primarily Grenache, Mourvèdre, Cinsault and Syrah for red wines, Roussanne and Viognier for white.

Key wines: Côte-Rôtie, Hermitage and **Crozes-Hermitage** in the north grow Syrah for robust, ageable reds (with Côte-Rôtie allowed to blend in a little Viognier for spice). Farther south, in its remarkably stony soil that retains the heat of the day and leads to deeper wines, **Châteauneuf-du-Pape** blends the major red varieties and as many as nine others into sturdy, sometimes distinguished and ageable wines. In the rolling hills surrounding Châteauneuf are vast vineyards growing these same grapes for fruity **Côtes-du-Rhône**, meant to be drunk early, and some districts that rise above the crowd, including **Gigondas** and **Vacqueyras**.

Key producers: Chapoutier, Jean-Louis Chave, Delas, Guigal, Jaboulet Aîné, Jasmin in the north. Beaucastel, Clos des Papes, Rayas, Vieux Télégraphe in the south.

Italy

From the foothills of the Alps in the north to sizzlingly hot Sicily in the south, Italy has as wide a climate range as any country in the world. Parts of Italy have made wine since before Roman times, but it did not become a single country until late in the 19th century. Its 20 culturally distinct regions retain their diversity to this day, so much so that each region could easily be a unique wine country.

If someone who knows a lot about Italian wine offers to share some discoveries with you, don't hesitate to accept.

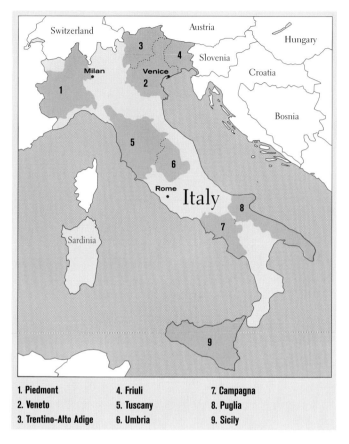

1. Piedmont
2. Veneto
3. Trentino-Alto Adige
4. Friuli
5. Tuscany
6. Umbria
7. Campagna
8. Puglia
9. Sicily

These wines are worth exploring in detail. What follows are the broad strokes.

Piedmont

Geography: The steep, rolling hills of this region have some of the most prized vineyards in Italy, mainly in the Barolo and Barbaresco districts. Generally, Nebbiolo gets the prime south-facing slopes, with the other grapes planted elsewhere. The hilltops are considered the best of the best, indicated with the word "Sorì" plus the vineyard name on the label.

Grapes: Nebbiolo, Dolcetto, Barbera for red; Cortese for dry white; Moscato for sweet white and sparkling. A full range of the classic French varieties—including Cabernet Sauvignon, Merlot, Chardonnay—are also grown here and bottled separately, usually under the grape name.

Key wines: Barolo and **Barbaresco** use Nebbiolo from prime, officially recognized vineyards, to make ageable reds that require two to four years of cellaring before release and up to 15 years before drinking. Other districts, such as **Gattinara** and **Ghemme**, make less celebrated reds from Nebbiolo, which is called **Spanna** there. Nebbiolo is also

made into an earlier-drinking red that carries a district designation, as in **Nebbiolo d'Alba**; the same districts grow Barbera and Dolcetto, as in **Barbera d'Alba** and **Dolcetto d'Asti**. **Gavi** is the prime district for dry white wine. **Moscato d'Asti** is a low-alcohol, sweet, lightly fizzy wine that is among the most charming dessert wines in the world. **Asti Spumante**, made from the same Moscato grape, is sweet and, like Champagne, fully sparkling.

Key producers: As in Burgundy, many of the very best wines are made by very small producers. Some of the larger high-quality wineries whose wines are most widely available are Ceretto, Gaja, Giacosa, Prunotto, Ratti, La Spinetta (Moscato).

Tuscany

Geography: The hills of Chianti cover the heart of Tuscany. Chianti Classico lies between Florence and Siena and has many of the highly regarded wines. Chianti Rufina lies to the northeast, Montalcino to the south. Bolgheri, a warmer region between Chianti and the sea, is the home of Sassicaia and several other high-profile Cabernet Sauvignon-based reds.

Grapes: Sangiovese, Caniolo and in some areas Cabernet Sauvignon for red wines; Trebbiano and Malvasia for white. Classic French varieties are bottled separately or blended with Sangiovese to make proprietary wines.

Key wines: Primarily red wines based on Sangiovese. Simple **Chianti** is just that, a simple quaff. More specific regional wines include **Chianti Classico, Chianti Rufina** (pronounced ROOF-ee-na), **Carmignano** (which permits a percentage of Cabernet Sauvignon in the blend), and especially **Brunello di Montalcino** (made from a local clone of Sangiovese called Brunello, it's among Italy's most ageable reds). Extra aging yields Riserva wines in each region—either alone or blended with local varieties—which often cost more than the traditional wines. Many also make *vin santo*, a sweet wine made by fermenting white grapes in a sealed cask.

Key producers: Ama, Antinori, Felsina Berardenga, Fonterutoli, Fontodi, Frescobaldi, Isole e Olena, Montevertine, Ruffino and Selvapiana in Chianti; Banfi, Biondi-Santi, Costanti and Poggio Antico in Montalcino; Avignonesi for Montepulciano and especially *vin santo*. Top proprietary wines, also known as "super Tuscans," include Sassicaia, Ornellaia and Argiano Solengo.

A note on oak: Until recently, traditional Tuscan (and indeed most Italian) reds were aged in large, neutral casks. Some producers, believing that this treatment destroyed freshness, started aging their wines for shorter periods in the smaller oak barrels used for Bordeaux, Burgundy and California wines. This retains freshness but also imparts the sweet tastes of vanilla and spice common to those other regions. Most proprietary wines get the barrel treatment, as does a significant percentage of Chianti. Most consumers like the results. Traditionalists vehemently call it heresy. (See "A Choice of Style," page 100.)

Northeastern Italy

Geography: As the wide, flat plain of the Po River begins its rise north toward the Alps, the hills, mountains and valleys create pockets of ideal conditions for certain kinds of amiable, easy-drinking wine. They begin around Lake Garda with **Bardolino**, stretch across the Veneto through the low hills of **Valpolicella** and **Soave**, and culminate in high vineyards that include **Alto Adige**, **Trentino** and **Friuli**. What all these wines have in common is lightness. They can be serious, but mostly they are abundant and drinkable early.

Grapes: Garganega and Trebbiano in Soave; Chardonnay, Pinot Bianco, Pinot Grigio, Sauvignon Blanc and Tocai Friulano elsewhere for white; Corvina and Rondinella in Valpolicella; Cabernet Franc, Merlot, Cabernet Sauvignon and Refosco elsewhere for reds.

Key wines: Mostly white wines, especially Soave and varietals in Friuli, Collio and Alto Adige. Most notable red is the light and refined Valpolicella. Grapes dried into raisins (called *passito*) make some of the most interesting wines, including Valpolicella's high-alcohol variant Amarone and super-sweet wines such as Recioto di Soave and Maculan's proprietary Torcolato. A few producers are making international-style blends based on Cabernet Sauvignon.

Key producers: Allegrini, Anselmi, Gini, Maculan, Masi, Pieropan in the Veneto; Grai, Lageder, Bollini, Ferrari (sparkling wine), Gravner, Jermann, Giovanni Puiatti, Schiopetto in the mountains.

Elsewhere in Italy

Geography: Between Piedmont in the northwest and Veneto in the northeast, the only pocket of serious wine is **Franciacorta**, which makes dry sparkling wines and some nice table wines in the low hills west of Milan. Between Tuscany and Rome are the rolling hills of Umbria, where the traditional wines, such as **Orvieto** and **Frascati**, are light whites. Farther south the weather becomes considerably warmer and favors big, sturdy wines with a different roster of grape varieties from anywhere else in Italy. This area will become increasingly important for good value wines and the occasional blockbuster.

Grapes: A long list, but the major ones in the south are Aglianico and Primitivo for red, Avellino and Greco di Tufo for white.

Key wines: Spumanti (sparkling wines) in Franciacorta; Orvieto and the proprietary wines of Antinori's Castello della Sala in Umbria; local white varietals and Taurasi (a red from Aglianico) in Campagna; Salice Salentino and Primitivo in Puglia.

Key producers: Bellavista and Ca' del Bosco in Franciacorta; Antinori's Castello della Sala and Palazzone in Umbria; Mastroberardino and Feudi di San Gregorio in Campagna; Taurino in Puglia; Corvo and Regaleali in Sicily.

Spain

The word on Spain used to be it was great if you liked old wine. Not only were the sherries brown in color; most of the red and white table wines were, too. No more. The worldwide trend toward freshness hit Spain in the 1990s. Current-vintage reds and, increasingly, whites, offer charms even Spanish-wine fans never knew were possible. Spain still makes some of the finest long-lived wines as well.

Spain exports dry wines in three categories: *crianza* (aged in wood for at least six months), *reserva* (aged in oak at least one year) and *gran reserva* (aged in wood at least two years). In practice, *gran reservas* are often aged three to seven years in oak barrels.

Rioja

Geography: In the center of northern Spain, at an altitude of 1,500 to 2,000 feet, this mountainous region gets more rain than most of Spain and therefore has wines with more delicacy.

Grapes: Tempranillo, Graciano and Garnacha (Grenache) for reds; Viura and Malvasia for whites.

Key wines: Rioja reds are the most widely available wines of Spain, often aged extensively (though in recent years for shorter periods) in American oak barrels. The whites, which for years were aged too long in oak, have become fresher, but they're still not distinguished.

Key producers: Contino, Marqués de Riscal, Martinez Bujanda, Remelluri, La Rioja Alta, CVNE.

Portugal	Spain	
1. Douro	1. Rioja	3. Penedès
2. Barraida	2. Ribera del Duero	4. Jerez
3. Dao		

Ribera del Duero

Geography: Ribera's hostile-looking flat landscape lies upriver from the region in Portugal that grows the grapes for Port. (Duero is Spanish for the same river that is the Douro in Portugal.) Hot and dry, the region gets abundant sun, which gives the wines their muscle.

Grapes: Traditional Spanish grapes Tempranillo and Garnacha (Grenache) mingle with Cabernet Sauvignon and Merlot.

Key wines: Ribera del Duero ranks among Spain's most illustrious reds for its powerful intensity and richness.

Key producers: Arroyo, Bodegas Alejandro Fernandez (Pesquera), Téofilo Reyes, Vega Sicilia.

Penedès

Geography: Tucked just below the Pyrenees, the region of Catalonia has its own culture. Penedès, not far south of the regional capital, Barcelona, is a picturesque area of gently rolling hills. Its wines seem to combine elements of French and Spanish wines.

Grapes: Parellada, Macabeo and Xarel-lo for white, plus French varieties for varietal wines.

Key wines: Sparkling wine, called cava, and dry table wine, usually identified by variety.

Key producers: Codorníu, Freixenet, Juve y Camps, J. Léon, Torres.

Jerez, the home of Sherry

Geography: Jerez is in the hot southwestern corner of Spain, on outcroppings that look like nothing more than dunes.

Grapes: Palomino is the main grape.

Key wines: Sherry, fortified with alcohol, comes in a range of styles. It starts out like a normal white wine, then undergoes a transformation in the aging process. Some styles develop a floating yeast, called *flor*, which introduces a pungent nutty flavor to the resulting wines: fino, the freshest, and amontillado, aged longer. Oloroso, a darker, richer wine, is free of *flor*. Palo Cortado blends fino and oloroso.

The solera: All sherry is aged in this unique system, in which barrels are stacked in tiers in the sun or in a warm room, which "cooks" the wine to its characteristic brown color and nutty, oxidized flavors. New wine goes into the top tier, and only a portion of the wine is taken from the bottom tier of barrels, which are then filled with wine from higher tiers. As a result, each bottle contains some wine from every vintage. Some soleras have been going for more than a century.

Key producers: Domecq, Gonzalez Byass, Harveys, Hidalgo, Lustau, Osborne, Valdespino.

Portugal

Geography: Although the country makes some good table wine, the action is in the steep hills fronting the Douro River, home of sweet, rich, alcoholically fortified Port.

Grapes: To make Port, Touriga and Tinta grapes are partially fermented; then enough clear, high-proof brandy is added to stop the fermentation, leaving plenty of unfermented sugar to sweeten the wine.

Key wines: Nonvintage types predominate, including ruby (red and sweet) and tawny (aged in oak barrels until its color becomes, well, tawny, and develops all kinds of nut and spice flavors). Both are drinkable on release. Vintage Port is made from the best vineyards in the best years, as declared by the individual producers. Bottled young, it wants 20 years or more of further aging. Late-Bottled Vintage (LBV) is aged longer before release and finished so it can be drunk upon release.

Key producers: Cockburn, Croft, Fonseca, Graham, Niepoort, Quinta do Noval, Smith Woodhouse, Taylor Fladgate, Warre.

Germany

If Riesling ever becomes popular again, America will rediscover German wine and find a trove of wonderful, elegant, refined whites. Until then, the enlightened among us can cherry-pick the really good ones. Contrary to popular belief, not all German wines are insipid and sweet. The best, in fact, have a racy juiciness that goes nicely with their delightful aromas.

Most German wines do have some sweetness, and German wine law carefully defines a series of categories

based on sweetness. Unfortunately, these categories reflect the sugar content of the grapes at harvest, not the amount of sweetness left in the bottle, which can vary greatly. Generally, however, the higher up the scale you go, the sweeter the finished wine will be. The categories, in ascending order, are: tafelwein, QbA (Qualitätswein bestimmer Anbaugebiete, which means quality wine from a specific region), Kabinett, Spätlese, Auslese, Beerenauslese, Eiswein and Trockenbeerenauslese. The last three are expensive dessert wines.

It has become increasingly common to identify the sweetness of the actual wine with the terms Trocken (dry) and Halbtrocken (off dry). Not all wines carry such helpful labels, although they meticulously spell out the region, vil-

The strikingly situated Kiedricher Gräfenberg vineyard, part of
the Robert Weil estate in the Rheingau.

lage and vineyard names in jawbreaking German.

Try not to let that deter you. The wines are much more
approachable than the labels.

Geography: The important vineyards cling to slopes fac-
ing the Rhine River and its tributaries. The weather is
cold, which makes the best wines crisp and zingy. The key
regions (and villages) for the better wines are:

- Mosel (Bernkastel, Erden, Graach, Piesport, Ürzig)
- Rheingau (Eltville, Johannisberg, Rüdesheim)
- Rheinhessen (Nackenheim, Nierstein, Oppenheim)
- Nahe (Niederhausen, Schlossböckelheim)
- Pfalz (Wachenheim, Deidesheim)

Grapes: Riesling, some Silvaner, Scheurebe (for sweet
wines).

Key producers: Bürklin-Wolf, Haag, Kloster Erbach,
Maximin Grünhaus, Gunderloch, Egon Müller, Müller-
Catoir, J.J. Prüm, Schloss Johannisberg, Schloss Vollrads,
von Kesseltatt, von Simmern.

Other Countries

Austria

Despite their similar German labels, Austria's wines are not much like Germany's, except for very sweet late-harvest wines. The predominant style is dry, even the Rieslings, which are fuller-bodied than their German counterparts. The Grüner Veltiner grape makes bracing, refreshing whites. Chardonnay, Sauvignon Blanc and Pinot Noir can be worthy. Late-harvest whites can equal Germany's.

Key producers: Alzinger, Brundlmeyer, Kracher, Prager.

Hungary

Best known for Tokaji, a distinctive sweet white wine. (See page 45.)

Switzerland

Few exceptional Swiss wines are made, and even fewer get to the U.S., but some can be fruity and agreeable.

The Essence

This chapter provides the necessary details on key U.S. regions (in particular California, the Pacific Northwest, New York, Virginia and Texas), South America, Australia, New Zealand and a few other countries whose wines are likely to be found in U.S. stores and restaurants.

NAPA VALLEY, CALIFORNIA.

The New World

California and the Pacific Northwest

Even though the west coast of the United States stretches some 1,500 miles, the wines grown in California, Oregon and parts of Washington have much in common, thanks to the profound influence of the Pacific Ocean and its chilly Alaska Current. The cool waters of the Pacific and prevailing winds blowing from the west keep the coastal climate temperate. Most of the coastline from Los Angeles to Seattle is mountainous, and where cooling fogs penetrate gaps in this coast range the mountain valleys are ideal for wine grapes.

Inland from the coast range, hotter conditions are better for everyday table wine than for fine wine, with two exceptions. Vineyards in the Sierra Nevada are high enough to experience the cooling influence of the mountains behind them. And Eastern Washington, a desert in the rain shadow of the Cascade Mountains, is far enough north and can pump enough water from the Columbia River and other underground sources to make exceptional wines. Similar conditions prevail in parts of Idaho and northeastern Oregon.

Oregon's main vineyards are in the coast range, which makes worthy Pinot Noir and Chardonnay in good vintages. The down side is that early autumn storms can spoil a vintage faster than you can say brown rot.

With few exceptions, the best west coast wines are varietals. Even most proprietary wines rely upon specific varietals. Opus One, for example, the famous Napa Valley collaboration of California's Robert Mondavi and Bordeaux's Philippine de Rothschild, only makes one wine; it contains enough Cabernet Sauvignon in most vintages to be labeled Cabernet Sauvignon, but it has more marketing cachet without the varietal name.

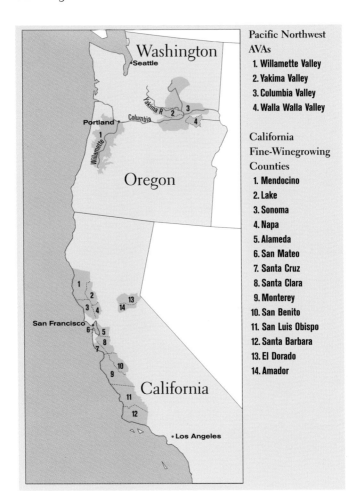

Pacific Northwest AVAs
1. Willamette Valley
2. Yakima Valley
3. Columbia Valley
4. Walla Walla Valley

California Fine-Winegrowing Counties
1. Mendocino
2. Lake
3. Sonoma
4. Napa
5. Alameda
6. San Mateo
7. Santa Cruz
8. Santa Clara
9. Monterey
10. San Benito
11. San Luis Obispo
12. Santa Barbara
13. El Dorado
14. Amador

Why this chapter is organized differently

At the wine shop or restaurant, American consumers ask for a Cabernet Sauvignon, not a Napa Valley red. Knowing where the grapes for that Cabernet Sauvignon were grown helps you to understand why it tastes as it does, and once you decide you want a Cabernet, you may want to narrow the choice to Napa Valley, or perhaps a district within Napa Valley. Experienced wine drinkers, however, choose a wine based upon the styles of individual wineries, even specific wines.

Infuriating as it may be to wine purists, if you ask 10 Americans with a glass of Columbia Crest Merlot in their hands where the wine came from, nine will say California. (It's in Washington.) To my mind, that means consumers accept Washington wines as readily as they do California wines. Is there a difference between Washington Merlot and California Merlot? You bet. Is it the first consideration? No. The first consideration is that it's a Merlot.

California and the Pacific Northwest really form one big region, because they have more in common with each other than with the rest of the United States. For that reason, the following section folds together the major west coast wine regions, all of which use the varietal system for naming their wines (give or take a few proprietary wines).

Cabernet Sauvignon

Napa Valley is ground zero for Cabernet in America. The overwhelming majority of the best Cabernets come from Napa Valley, and their prices usually reflect that. A classic Napa Valley Cabernet is a dense wine with rich flavors centering on black currant and other dark fruits, often with a characteristic tinge of an herbal overlay. Styles range from silky to plush to bitingly tannic.

Other regions produce wonderful Cabernet, including:

- Sonoma Valley, California (often dense, tannic)

- Alexander Valley, California (often supple with a strong herbal component)

- Santa Cruz Mountains, California (one great vineyard: Ridge's Monte Bello)

- Paso Robles, California (supple, round)

- Columbia Valley, Washington (marked by pure fruit character)

Key producers: Arrowood, Beringer, Caymus, Chateau St. Jean, Chateau Ste. Michelle, Columbia Crest, Diamond Creek, Dunn, Flora Springs, Hess Collection, R. Mondavi, Opus One, Phelps, Ridge, Stag's Leap Wine Cellars.

Merlot

Those regions that do well with Cabernet often do as well with Merlot, which has similar characteristics but less density. Washington succeeds more consistently with this grape than California does. The best Merlots from Washington are characteristically rich in fruit flavor, often augmented by more than a hint of spicy oak.

Other regions:

- Napa Valley, California (often as tough as Cabernet when young)

- Sonoma Valley, California (distinctly softer and silkier)

Key producers: Arrowood, Beringer Howell Mountain, Cuvaison, Columbia Crest, Chateau Ste. Michelle, Leonetti, Matanzas Creek, Pride Mountain.

Pinot Noir

Today's American Pinot often celebrates the grape's berry and plum flavors, and the best regions produce wines that capture seductive textures and flavors reminiscent of the best

Burgundies. Russian River Valley in Sonoma County can achieve the headiest fruit flavors and silkiest textures in the U.S.

Other regions:

- Carneros, California (spicy, often delicate)

- Santa Ynez Valley, California (more red fruits than black, sometimes herbal)

- Willamette Valley, Oregon (exceedingly supple and refined)

Key producers: Acacia, Au Bon Climat, Beaux Frères, Dehlinger, Domaine Drouhin, Ponzi, Saintsbury, Sanford, Williams-Selyem.

Zinfandel

Zinfandel grows virtually everywhere in California. In the hot Central Valley it makes the raw material for white Zinfandel. The best red Zinfandels come from the warmer parts of coastal valleys. Those places that are just a bit too warm for great Cabernet often make sensational Zinfandel.

Best regions:

- Dry Creek Valley, California (classic berry with tarry overtones)

- Alexander Valley, California (ripe, heady wines)

- Paso Robles, California (more cherry than berry)

- Napa Valley, California (especially around Calistoga and in the mountains; rich and dense)

- Mount Veeder, California (dense, complex)

Key producers: Kenwood, Preston, Rafanelli, Ravenswood, Ridge, Sky, Turley.

Chardonnay

California and Washington excel at making large quantities of Chardonnay blended from several regions. At the expensive end of the scale, however, the most distinguished wines come from individual regions and often specific vineyards in the cooler areas. Many fine California Chardonnays

come from Carneros—a very cool growing region that strad-
dles the southern portions of Napa and Sonoma counties—
and from those parts of Napa and Sonoma that are closest to
it, and therefore relatively cool. These wines have the crucial
balance of richness with enough acidity (from the cool climate) to make complex wines with great finesse.

Other regions:

- Russian River Valley, California (similar to Carneros)

- Alexander Valley, California (creamy, heady styles)

- Anderson Valley, California (abundant fruit flavors and
  delicacy)

- Santa Barbara County, California (earthy, complex)

- Columbia Valley, Washington (lively acidity balanced
  with abundant fruit)

- Willamette Valley, Oregon (new plantings yielding
  most flavorful wines)

Key producers: Argyle, Au Bon Climat, Beringer, Chalk
Hill, Chalone, Chateau Ste. Michelle, Columbia Crest,
Ferrari-Carano, Kistler, Matanzas Creek, R. Mondavi,
Pine Ridge, Saintsbury, Sanford, Sonoma-Cutrer,
Woodward Canyon.

Sauvignon Blanc

California and Washington seem to do everything possible
to tame the wilder aspects of this variety, including overcrop-
ping to dim the flavors and barrel fermentation and aging to
cover them. More than any other wine type, Sauvignon
Blanc depends on the winemaker's stylistic choices.

Key producers: Those that celebrate the natural pungency
of the grape include Babcock, Brander, Mayacamas,
Sanford, Rochioli, Voss and Geyser Peak. Others, including Caymus and Chalk Hill, take rich, barrel-fermented
white Bordeaux as their models.

Sparkling

As in Champagne, the best regions in the U.S. for making sparkling wine are the coldest. The idea is to ripen the grapes without losing too much acidity or picking up too much color. Not surprisingly, the best places for Chardonnay and Pinot Noir table wine also excel at sparkling wine; Carneros is home to several of California's finest fizz makers.

Other regions:

- Anderson Valley, California (home to Roederer Estate and Pacific Echo, formerly Scharffenberger)

- Sonoma-Green Valley, California (home to Iron Horse)

- Santa Barbara, California (home to Maison Deutz)

- Columbia Valley, Washington (home to Domaine Ste. Michelle)

- Willamette Valley, Oregon (home to Argyle)

Other key producers: Domaine Carneros, Codorniu Napa, Domaine Chandon, Domaine Mumm, Gloria Ferrer and Mountain Dome.

The Rest of the U.S.

New York

Long Island, historically an agricultural region best known for potatoes, has found some success with Chardonnay and Merlot. Up north in the Finger Lakes region, careful viticulture and enology can yield juicy Rieslings, occasionally in late-harvest styles. Availability is limited.

Key producers: Lenz, Palmer and Pindar on Long Island; Fox Run, Dr. Konstantin Frank and Lamoreaux Landing in the Finger Lakes.

Virginia

The foothills of the Appalachians in the western part of the state grow Chardonnay and Riesling that can be stylish.

Key producers: Barboursville, Prince Michel, Piedmont.

Texas

Texas hill country, in the middle of the state between Austin and San Antonio, looks and feels like wine country, and the far southwestern corner of the state has extensive vineyards, but the best Chardonnay and Cabernet come from the flat plains around Midland-Odessa.

Key producers: Cap Rock, Fall Creek, Llano Estacado, Messina Hof, Pheasant Ridge.

VIÑA SAN PEDRO, CHILE.

South America

Argentina

Mendoza is the major region. Its red wine, made from Malbec, has a soft texture and easy drinkability.

Key producers: Bodegas Esmeralda, Catena, Trapiche.

Chile

An influx of investment from North America and Europe has speeded up development of this already-established wine producing country. It has been most successful with moderate-priced wines made from familiar grape varieties.

A long slender central valley stretches north and south from Chile's capitol of Santiago and includes Maipo, a warm region that makes good Cabernet Sauvignon, and

Rapel, notable mainly for its ripe, sometimes luscious Merlot. Casablanca, a cooler region on the coast, is known for its juicy Chardonnays and tangy Sauvignon Blancs.

Almaviva and Seña are two promising high-profile joint ventures to make high-end reds.

Key producers: Carmen, Casa Lapostolle, Concha y Toro (which makes Almaviva with Mouton), Errazuriz (which makes Seña with Mondavi), Montes, Santa Rita.

Australia

In this huge country, the wine regions are separated by hundreds of miles. That doesn't stop the big wineries from blending wines from all over into remarkably pleasing blends with the appellations "Australia" or "Southeastern Australia." Some of these rank among the best wine values in the world, consistently delivering pleasure for the dollar.

The big wineries' cross-appellation blends can even be mind-bendingly delicious and distinguished. But the majority of Australia's small wineries are just as deeply rooted in their own small regions as those of any winegrowing country. A brand-new system of appellations was wending its way through the development and approval process in the late 1990s. What follows is a brief sketch of the key regions for top-quality wines.

THE HILL OF GRACE VINEYARD AT HENSCHKE IN SOUTH AUSTRALIA.

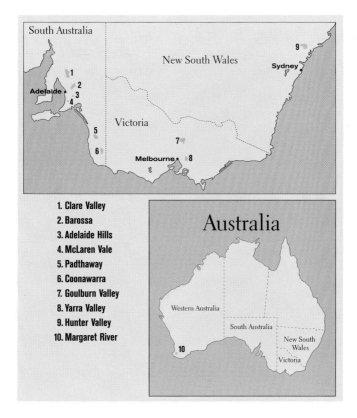

1. Clare Valley
2. Barossa
3. Adelaide Hills
4. McLaren Vale
5. Padthaway
6. Coonawarra
7. Goulburn Valley
8. Yarra Valley
9. Hunter Valley
10. Margaret River

South Australia

The state of South Australia is Australia's wineland, with the majority of the nation's vineyards. Many of them are in the vast Riverland region one low mountain range away from the hot, red Outback. Around Adelaide on the seacoast are several regions with a long history of producing some of Australia's finest.

- **Barossa:** Warm region with many old vineyards that make extra-ripe, exotic Shiraz.
  Key producers: Henschke (reds), Peter Lehmann, St. Hallett.

- **McLaren Vale:** Vines carpet low, rolling hills that make Shiraz tasting of fresh fruit.

Key producers: Chateau Reynella, Hardys, Rosemount (Syrah), Seaview, Wirra Wirra.

- **Adelaide Hills:** The coolest climate in the region makes distinguished Chardonnays.
Key producers: Henschke (whites), Lenswood, Petaluma, Shaw & Smith.

- **Clare Valley:** Chalky soils yield a crisp style of Shiraz and aromatic dry Rieslings.
Key producers: Grosset, Leasingham, Jim Barry, Pikes.

- **Coonawarra:** A flat outcropping of limestone on a flat plain grows Cabernet Sauvignons of distinction.
Key producers: Katnook, Lindemans (esp. Limestone Ridge), Penley, Rosemount (Cabernet), Wynns Coonawarra Estate.

- **Padthaway:** This geographic cousin of Coonawarra seems to do best with Chardonnay.
Key producers: Hardys, Lindemans, Orlando.

Elsewhere in Australia

Victoria

The coolest wine regions in continental Australia cluster around Melbourne in proximity to Port Philip Bay, which opens onto the Tasman Sea. Picture-book **Yarra Valley** is the best known of several regions—including **Geelong** and **Mornington Peninsula**—that do best with Chardonnay and the occasional Pinot Noir. In the low mountains that separate these regions from the broiling Outback, pockets of vineyards in **Great Western**, **Goulburn Valley**, **Macedon** and **Pyrenees** do particularly well with Shiraz. Rutherglen is best known for its luscious dessert wines.

Key producers: Bannockburn, Coldstream Hills, Mitchelton, Morris, Scotchmans Hill, Seppelt, Yalumba.

New South Wales

Hunter Valley has a reputation all out of proportion to its size due to its proximity to Sydney, Australia's largest city. Good wines do come from the Hunter, particularly Chardonnay and a distinctive style of Sémillon that ages well. Developments in the cooler climates of the Great Dividing Range promise much.

Key producers: Lindemans, Rosemount, Tyrrells.

Western Australia

Small regions south of Perth in the southwestern corner of the continent, including **Margaret River** and **Great Southern**, have some of the country's most temperate and consistent weather. So far, only Chardonnay and the occasional Riesling are of international interest.

Key producers: Goundrey, Leeuwin, Moss Wood, Pierro.

New Zealand

Geography: New Zealand has what appears to be the ideal *terroir* for Sauvignon Blanc in its **Marlborough** region, farther south than, and therefore cooler than, Australia. It's at the north end of the cooler South Island. A string of mountains runs along the north-south backbone of the country, creating pockets of interesting microclimates that favor different varieties. Whites are more successful than reds.

Grapes: Sauvignon Blanc, Chardonnay and Riesling are the major whites. Pinot Noir and Merlot are the major reds, with some Cabernet Sauvignon.

Key wines: Sauvignon Blanc from Marlborough and Chardonnay from several regions are the stars. Juicy Rieslings are worth noting. Reds tend to be overpriced.

Key producers: Brancott (known as Montana in New Zealand), Cloudy Bay, Giesen, Goldwater, Jackson Estate, Matua, Morton, Te Mata, Wairau River.

Other countries

Canada

Long thought too cold to make decent wine, Canada has two regions that can surprise you. Okanagan Valley in British Columbia, near Vancouver, can ripen Chardonnay and Riesling effectively. The best red is Lemberger. The Niagara Peninsula, which juts into Lake Erie, makes stunning ice wines from Riesling and Pinot Gris.

Key producers: Inniskillin, Mission Hill.

QUALITY WINEMAKING IN ISRAEL HAS EXPANDED IN RECENT YEARS.

Israel

Not just for kosher wine drinkers, Israel's wineries have improved of late and make some drinkable wines from major varietals in the country's warm climate.

Key producers: Golan Heights, Yarden.

Lebanon

Chateau Musar, in the war-torn Bekaa Valley, makes one of the quirkiest, funkiest red wines in the world.

South Africa

Vineyards cluster near Cape Town, on the Atlantic coast. Sauvignon Blancs, especially those from Thelema, and the occasional Shiraz, especially Saxenburg's, merit attention. The workhorse grapes of the country's wines are Chenin Blanc for whites and Pinotage, a cross of Pinot Noir and Cinsault, which has neither the charm of the former nor the personality of the latter.

The Essence

This chapter explores some of the ramifications of geography and grape varieties that come up in wine conversations again and again.

For example, *terroir*, a French word for all those factors about a vineyard site that are not controllable by man, includes soil, climate, the contour of the land and other environmental elements. The better the wine, the more important *terroir* is.

Because appellation systems vary from one part of the world to another, knowing what they mean can help you sidestep some nasty traps. Vintage charts are most useful if you know how to interpret them. Is modern winemaking destroying traditional wines by making wines drinkable earlier? The evidence says otherwise.

CHAPTER FIVE

Putting It in Perspective

The terror of *terroir*

You can't talk about wine for very long without someone bringing up the issue of *terroir*. The definition is simple enough: all those factors about a vineyard site that are not controllable by man. The implications are much trickier.

Some wine experts translate *terroir* as simply "soil," which is misleading. This mistake probably comes from bandying about the French phrase "*goût de terroir*" (taste of *terroir*), which somehow got itself attached to earthy, often dirty flavors in wines. A more accurate meaning of *terroir* is "environment." That includes the soil in which the vines are planted, but it also comprises climate, the contour of the land and any other environmental factor you can imagine. All of these affect the wine.

Certain sites stand out for making particularly good wines or bad wines within the same region. For example, a vineyard that tilts toward the sun will ripen grapes faster and more evenly than a vineyard next door that tilts in another direction. A vineyard with densely packed clay soil will encourage more foliage and put less energy into ripening fruit than a vineyard in the same climate with stony, easily drained soil. Certain minerals in one vineyard's soil make for softer wine than another's.

In places with a long history, such as Burgundy, these specifics solidify into something resembling a code. The wines from Beaune Grèves should have a richer texture and darker flavors than those from Beaune Vignes Franches—just a few yards away—which should be more elegant and floral, even though both vineyards grow the same Pinot Noir grapes.

Experts can become so thoroughly familiar with the wines from these vineyards that they can taste them blind

DIAMOND CREEK VINEYARDS BOASTS THREE DIFFERENT SOIL TYPES WHICH
PRODUCE THREE DIFFERENT VINEYARD-DESIGNATED WINES: RED ROCK
TERRACE (LEFT) GRAVELLY MEADOW (MIDDLE) AND VOLCANIC HILL (RIGHT).

and identify the source a large percentage of the time. But
that requires years of study, sort of the way a longtime football fan can pick up a subtle shift in blocking patterns. To
the rest of us, it's just chaos.

The reason is that *terroir* competes with some powerful
factors in the finished wine. Vintage differences blur the
effects of *terroir*, and winemaking can manipulate these
fragile characteristics in many directions.

A warm year, for example, can make a vineyard known
to produce delicate wines yield richer, sturdier wines than
usual. A wet year can dilute these characteristics. A winemaker who chooses to harvest late and ferment the wine cold
will make a wine very different from one who picks early and
ferments warm. And these are just two of the dozens of ways
a winemaker can influence the finished wine.

Sensitive winemakers try to amplify the natural characteristics of *terroir*. Aging on the lees might produce flavors
reminiscent of hazelnuts in wine from one site, while the
same technique applied to wine from another site might
introduce a subtle coffee flavor. Without aging on the lees,
neither flavor would appear, and the wine would be less
complex and reflect its *terroir* less distinctly.

Wines from certain sites pick up flavors from oak aging more readily than others made from the same grape variety in the same region. A winemaker can use that knowledge to shorten the aging process and minimize the oak flavor in the wine, or let it age a little longer to reflect this influence.

Talented winemakers learn how to balance these effects, just as an orchestra conductor might make sure that the brass and woodwinds don't overpower the strings when everyone is playing together. Think of it this way. Each grape variety has its own set of characteristics, just as a trumpet will sound like a trumpet whether it plays the music of Bach or Basie. The *terroir*, the place where the grape grows, is the music. Bach will sound like Bach whether a trumpet or a violin is playing it. Just as certain music sounds better when certain instruments play it, certain *terroirs* express themselves more with certain grape varieties.

Appellations and hierarchies

Most of the world puts appellations on wine labels to tell us where the wine came from. In France and Italy, however, wine laws take things a few steps further and permit only certain grape varieties and certain viticultural and winemaking practices. These can be useful in understanding the wines of a region, but don't make the mistake of thinking that appellation laws exist for consumer protection. Historically, the rules were invented to protect wine producers.

France put its Appellation d'Origine Contrôlée (AOC) system in place in the 1930s to protect responsible wine-growers from rampant cheating by competitors. In effect, the laws spelled out where and how the wines were to be made so that cheaters could not sneak in wines from else-where or dilute the integrity of the place names by stretch-ing the appellations beyond reason.

The law codified practices that responsible vintners were already using, including a hierarchy of vineyard sites. In Burgundy, it identified certain sites that could use the titles *grand cru* (for the best) and *premier cru* (for the next tier). It specified maximum yields in the vineyard and permitted only certain grape varieties in certain regions.

That all sounds good, but the system contained some loopholes. Until the 1980s, for example, some Burgundians took advantage of a slick deal known as the "cascade" sys-tem. Unscrupulous producers simply bottled excess wine from their *grand cru* vineyards as lesser wines. This allowed them to make thin and insipid wines, sell the maximum volume permitted as expensive *grand cru* and sell the rest under lesser appellations. These days, any vintner that makes more than he should from a specific vineyard must declassify the whole thing. (They can still legally inflate the permitted yields by a percentage that changes from year to year—less obvious and less destructive, but still...)

The bottom line, however, is that AOC worked by bring-ing a measure of confidence to a wine industry that had been touched by scandal.

Italy picked up on France's success with AOC with its own version, called Denominazione d'Origine Controllata (DOC). Like France, Italy codified existing practices, draw-ing boundaries around regions and districts and specifying what grapes could be grown where and how. But Italy had not advanced as far as France, and later found it necessary to add another tier, called Denominazione d'Origine Controllata e Garantita (DOCG), with stricter regulations and a taste-approval process.

One quirk of Italy's system is that, until very recently, it did not even recognize some of the country's greatest wines. For example, super Tuscans — made from grape varieties or techniques not approved for their appellations — had to carry the same designation (*vino da tavola*) as the cheapest, least distinctive wines. They were easy to spot, however, by their price tags. Now these wines come under a classification called Indicazione Geographica Tipica (IGT) which at least tells you which region produced the wine.

THIS SOIL PROFILE FROM THE MAIPO VALLEY, CHILE, SHOWS HOW ROCKY SOME GRAPEGROWING SOIL CAN BE.

Italy continues to tinker with its DOC/DOCG system. Meanwhile, there has been an overall improvement in the country's wines.

But whether it's France's AOC or Italy's DOC, the implication is that wines higher up in the hierarchy are better than the rest, when the truth is that lollygaggers, miscreants and incompetents make a mockery of any system. In short, a simple Bourgogne from a good producer in Burgundy will always be a better wine than a Corton from a bad producer, even though the Corton could cost five to ten times as much.

Geographical appellation systems elsewhere in Europe have their own quirks. Germany's, for example, adds a layer of rules about the sweetness of the grapes at harvest. Outside Europe, appellation systems deal almost entirely with geography; they don't specify grape varieties or viticultural methods. In the U.S., American Viticultural Areas draw boundaries around appellations. Australia's new system, called Geographical Indications, imposes a more all-embracing hierarchy of regions, districts and sub-districts.

Any hierarchical system, however, is far more likely to be valid within a winery's own output than it will in the world at large. The message for us is: First, find a good producer.

Vintages and vintage charts

The most obvious reason to know what year a wine was made is to know how old it is. The vintage on the label provides that basic information. But it can tell us even more.

How's the weather in your neighborhood? Does it change from year to year? Of course it does. So do conditions at a vineyard site. Some years are cooler, some are wetter, occasionally one is perfect. Every change in the weather affects the grapevine's natural cycle—which ultimately affects the wine made from it.

BESIDES THE SOIL THAT GRAPES GROW IN, THE CONCEPT OF TERROIR INCLUDES THE CLIMATE AND THE CONTOUR OF THE LAND.

If we know what the weather was like in the place where the grapes were grown, the vintage on the label gives us a broad clue about the wine inside. If it was a warm year, we can expect the wine to taste ripe and generous. If it is was a cold year, we can brace ourselves for a more austere wine.

That's the point of vintage charts. They rate the overall quality of specific regions in specific years. And if every vineyard and every vintner did equally well, vintage charts would be a perfect tool for choosing a wine. Alas, every region has its underachievers, and a good vintage does not always guarantee a good wine.

Smart consumers also know that, even in fair and poor vintages, some producers always overcome the adversity of weather to make better wine than their cohorts. Seek out these wines, for two reasons. First, if prices are down overall because of a weak vintage, these wines often represent excellent value. And second, if other consumers are ignoring the vintage, you might be able to find bottles from good producers whose wines disappear from the shelves fast in better vintages.

That said, be aware that poor-to-middling vintages have that reputation for a reason. Don't expect the wines from these years to age as well or as long as the best wines from the best vintages. The general rule is to enjoy them while they are young rather than take the chance that they will fall apart with age.

Vintage has another meaning in reference to Port and Champagne; most of these wines are non-vintage and only the best years are bottled separately. This is where the term "a vintage year" denotes something specific.

A choice of style

Welcome to one of the evergreen arguments of wine: namely, are new-fangled ideas ruining traditional wines or making them better?

Take Piedmont as an example, mainly because it stirs up the fiercest emotions in its wines' partisans. The Nebbiolo grape grown there is naturally high in tannin. To make a drinkable wine from Nebbiolo requires some savvy wine-making. For generations, winemakers extended fermentations as long as they could to extract as much flavor as they could, then aged the wine in big, neutral casks for as much as seven or eight years to get the tannins to drop out. Often, these wines tasted oxidized and bereft of any fruit character.

In the 1980s, a small group of winemakers in Barolo and Barbaresco tried a different approach. They limited yields in the vineyard in order to ripen the grapes more evenly and produce less harsh tannins. They shortened fermentation times to extract less tannin, which in turn meant the wines required less aging to become balanced for drinking.

This scandalized the traditionalists. How dare they change the taste of the wines? Barolo, they said, is not supposed to taste of fruit and feel supple. Where are the tannins? Where are the extra dimensions of earthy flavor that come from long aging?

The same sort of argument has played out in other prominent regions. In Burgundy, the riper, fuller style of the modernists was pooh-poohed by traditionalists who praised the silky refinement of the previous generation's lean and less generous wines. In Spain, the density and intensity of modern wines tasted all wrong to traditionalists accustomed to older, extra-woody wines.

The first skirmishes in the modern-vs.-traditional battle were fought in Bordeaux, when several of the best known châteaus started making their wines softer and more supple. "They'll never age," grumped the traditionalists, who believed that wines needed to taste rough and harsh when they were young in order to taste smooth and delicious when they were old.

Well, that battle is all

but over. You can drink today's Bordeaux reds—even the first growths—without grimacing when they are three to five years old. A few traditionalists still grouch that the winemakers are pandering to those who don't want to bother cellaring their wines, but the evidence is in the bottle. At 15 to 20 years, the earliest Bordeaux reds made in this new style are doing just fine. Those non-traditional Barolos and Barbarescos from the mid-1980s are drinking just fine at the turn of the century, too, and the Burgundies are doing at least as well.

I don't believe that wine must be hard to drink when it is young in order to be good when it matures. Besides, while the traditionalists wait 15 or 20 years for their purchases to "come around," as they used to say, the rest of us can enjoy the wines young, old and in-between.

The Essence

Matching a wine to the occasion is more important than matching it to the food, and easier. Save serious wines for formal evenings, or for get-togethers with others who share a passion for wine.

The key to choosing a wine to go with food is to consider sweetness and acidity. If the food is sweet, choose a soft (low-acid) wine. If the food is tart, go for a wine high in acidity. If the food is neither sweet nor tart, drink anything you like. Most people prefer lighter wines with delicate food, heavier wines with more robust food.

Although glasses come in various shapes and sizes designed for specific wines, you can serve anything in a 10- to 12-ounce all-purpose glass. Don't get hung up on letting wine breathe; just pour it and let it be exposed to air in everyone's glass. Store leftover wine for a couple of days in the refrigerator, or for up to a week using an inert-gas system. For long-term storage, try freezing it. Thaw at room temperature or in the microwave.

In a restaurant, the most important thing to look for in the tasting ritual is temperature; most wine wants to be cool, not cold. If the wine is too warm or too cold, say so. Then take your time approving the taste.

CHAPTER SIX

Serving Wine

On a sultry August evening, with the warm sun hanging high in the sky at dinnertime, no wine is likely to taste better than a refreshing Riesling, juicy with citrusy acidity, pretty fruit flavors and floral aromas. To drink a serious, complex, mature Chardonnay at that moment would be like showing up in white tie and tails.

In their enthusiasm over newfound treasures, newcomers to wine often choose one without considering that serious wines deserve careful attention. If you pay big money for a wine, you want to get all you can out of it, and that means drinking it in a setting in which it's OK to pay attention to it at the table. A casual setting, unless you're in the company of fellow wine aficionados, does

Some warm weather wines	Some cold weather wines
Champagne and sparkling wine	California Chardonnay
Riesling	Viognier
Sauvignon Blanc (but not barrel-fermented)	Sauvignon Blanc (barrel-fermented)
Friuli Pinot Bianco, Pinot Grigio, Traminer	Alsace Gewürztraminer
Chablis	White Burgundy
Dolcetto	Barolo
Côtes du Rhône Village	Côte-Rôtie
Beaujolais	Red Burgundy
Moscato d'Asti	Port

Casual wines	Serious occasion wines
Generic white	Chardonnay
Pouilly-Fuissé	Meursault
Muscadet	Pouilly-Fumé
Chianti	Chianti Classico Riserva
Nebbiolo d'Alba	Barolo or Barbaresco
Château Larose-Trintaudon	Château Léoville-Las Cases
Rosemount Diamond Label Shiraz	Rosemount Balmoral Syrah
Asti Spumante	Rutherglen Liqueur Muscat

not lend itself to focusing attention on the wine. The time to open a serious wine is when there's a chill in the air and serious food on the table.

There are wines that manage to be complex, elegant and serious and, at the same time, easily approachable and smooth to drink. Fortunately, you don't need to find such a rarity if you just match the wine to the occasion.

Wine with food: Making it simple

Like any pastime, matching wine and food can become an obsession. If that's not your style, don't worry. Understanding a few basic ideas can improve your odds of making wine and food do a nice little dance on your palate.

I liken it to stereo equipment. You can slap a CD in the slot of a basic system and let it play. Or you can adjust the dynamic equalization to just the right curve and place the speakers just so, until the sound balances just right for your ears. In this chapter, I offer a few essential ideas. Later, in Chapter 9, I take the stereophile approach.

The big secrets

I used to think that the way to match food and wine was to choose wines whose flavors don't clash with the food. I came up with all sorts of fine-sounding theories, such as the reason Chardonnay tastes so good with mustard-sauced chicken is because of the honey flavors in the Chardonnay (as in honey-mustard dressing). Certainly, those flavors do taste good together, but what makes a match work has little to do with specific flavors and everything to do with a few basic elements.

In wine, the keys are sweetness, acidity and tannin. Most table wines are dry rather than sweet, so that element comes into play less often than the others. You need ask only two questions of most wines:

(1) How tart or soft is it?
(2) How tannic is it?

In food, most people recognize four basic tastes: sweet, sour, salty and bitter. For wine-matching purposes, salty and bitter are not critical (unless they are way off the scale).

- Sweetness counts because sweet foods make dry wines taste sour and thin. Better to drink wine with some sweetness of its own to balance sweet foods.

- Acidity (sourness) counts, too, because tart foods (such as those with lots of vinegar or citrus in them) react with the acidity in wine to make the wine taste softer. A wine that tastes balanced by itself can seem sweet and flabby next to a dish with tartness. On the other hand, a wine naturally high in acidity comes into balance next to the same dish.

There is one more element in food that affects wine profoundly. It's called *umami*. Discovered almost a century ago by Japanese scientists, it is the fifth taste. Almost a century before that, the French culinary philosopher Brillat-Savarin, in his seminal book, *The Physiology of Taste*, wrote extensively about a "savory" taste. I believe it to be the same thing. Foods high in *umami* include oysters, tomatoes, mushrooms, consommés and long-braised meat.

For matching purposes, all you need to know about *umami* is that it emphasizes tannin in wine. That's why the traditional wines to serve with oysters are white and not oaky (because oak has tannins) and the wines to serve with braised lamb are mature reds in which the tannins have softened from long aging.

Once you get these basic elements in line, you can play the flavor game. Go ahead, choose a Sauvignon Blanc with lots of herb flavor to go with that fish with an herb sauce. Pick a smoky Zinfandel to accompany that grilled steak. It works, so long as the keys balance.

THE 10 MOST FOOD-FRIENDLY WINES
Alsace Tokay/Pinot Gris
Italian Pinot Bianco
New Zealand Sauvignon Blanc
Muscadet (or Melon from California)
Riesling from anywhere
Barbera from anywhere
Chianti (but not riserva)
Washington Merlot
Pinot Noir from California or Oregon
Châteauneuf-du-Pape

These wines are slam dunks with a wide variety of foods because they tend to be neither too acidic nor too soft, and

because they stay away from tannin—including tannin from long oak aging of the white wines—which can clash with food. Other wines can be delicious with food, but the range of styles within a category can play dirty tricks on the unsuspecting. Zinfandel, for example, can be racy and fruity, much like Barbera or Chianti, but it can also be big and mighty, like a grand Cabernet Sauvignon, which needs wine-friendly food for best effect, such as ...

THE 6 MOST WINE-FRIENDLY FOODS
Roast chicken
Roast beef (not too well done)
Roast lamb (ditto)
Spaghetti with oil and tomato
Roasted or broiled halibut
Parmigiano-Reggiano cheese

The magic food to serve whenever you have a dry table wine to show off—red, white or rosé—is simple roast chicken. I have never known a wine to fail with it, and most wines inevitably taste better because of its presence. (Roast turkey with gravy does equally well, but beware the sweet side dishes surrounding it on Thanksgiving.)

For red wines, roast beef and roast lamb are classics. Most Bordeaux and Burgundy lovers insist their favorite red wines taste best with one or the other. Any simple pasta dish can be a tabula rasa for wine so long at it has no strong flavors. Halibut, without any strong character of its own, prepared with no extra flavors, goes splendidly with virtually any wine (red as well as white). And Parmigiano is the rare cheese that harms no wine.

An analogy for the fashion-conscious

Here's another way to think of the right-wine-with-food question. Imagine a fashion-conscious woman opening her closet door and, having selected a dress, considering which accessories to match with them. She might pass up her favorite scarf or purse in favor of ones that look best with the dress. When she does it well, her friends will notice how good she looks.

Some women go to great lengths to choose things that look fabulous together. Others couldn't care less, and they grab the first things that look decent. Which is "right"? The answer depends on how much you care about style. Whatever you choose is a reflection of your taste, and that's what counts. Fashion mavens might quarrel with that statement, just as food-and-wine mavens might argue that the details of a food-and-wine match matter profoundly. I say it's up to you to decide how much attention to invest in it. If you do develop a strong interest, be sure to check out Chapter 11 for more on this subject.

Glasses: choices, choices

The size, shape and quality of wineglasses definitely affect the pleasure you can get from drinking wine. Try it yourself. Pour the same wine into any two glasses of differing size and shape. The differences are most obvious if one glass is smaller than usual and the other larger, or if the shapes are markedly unlike. Sometimes the contents can seem like two different wines.

The best glasses are made of clear, thin crystal, with a generous capacity of 10 ounces or more and a tulip or globe-shaped bowl that curves in at the top to concentrate the aromas. Wineglasses have long stems so you can hold them without touching the bowl. In general, the bigger the bowl, the more powerful the aromas—as long as the opening is relatively small—but also the quicker the wine warms in the glass. So red wines get large bowls to enhance bouquet, while white wines get smaller ones to keep the wine cool.

One glassmaker, Riedel, takes glass design to extremes. Georg Riedel has devoted years of experimentation to determine an ideal glass shape for each type of wine. His theory is that certain shapes emphasize certain aromas, and manipulating the size and contour of the glass can guide more of the liquid to different parts of the mouth. In theory, one shape can emphasize acidity while another minimizes the effect of tannin. It sounds complicated and obscure, but I am convinced it does work.

SPECIALTY GLASSES FROM RIEDEL'S SOMMELIERS COLLECTION (LEFT TO RIGHT): BOURGOGNE, LOIRE, CHAMPAGNE, AND VINTAGE PORT

That said, I don't believe anyone needs an arsenal of glass sizes and shapes to enjoy wine any more than one needs a $25,000 high-end audio system to listen to the latest Mariah Carey CD. A good all-purpose glass of at least 10 ounces can handle anything.

Specialty shapes

The one-shape-fits-all theory is practical and prudent, but it's also true that specialty wines do much better with certain glasses. The most obvious is sparkling wine. The classic Champagne flute, a tall, narrow, elongated glass, holds a generous serving while minimizing the surface area, thus preventing the wine from releasing its bubbles too quickly.

In Bordeaux, they drink their red wine from tulip-shaped glasses. In Burgundy, you will get your wine in a spherical glass. This no mere caprice. These shapes actually show off the best aspects of the respective wines. If you drink a significant amount of Burgundy or Pinot Noir, invest in a set of appropriate glasses, ideally somewhat larger than the 10-ounce Bordeaux glass. Trust me, some wines do taste better in a fish bowl-sized glass, especially Barolo and Syrah wines.

Ports and sherries, powerful as they are, seem to like smaller glasses, not tiny thimbles but glasses that hold maybe five to six ounces. Aromatic table wines—especially German and Alsace wines and their New World counterparts Riesling, Pinot Gris and Pinot Blanc—also like smaller glasses, especially ones with long stems so you won't warm the wine by touching the bowl of the glass.

Lead crystal

The thinner the rim of the glass, the better the wine will taste, and lead crystal stemware is normally thinner and more brilliant than regular glass. Other glass mixtures produce a more brittle product. There has been some concern over how much lead can leach into wine from glass. I doubt that drinking wine out of lead crystal glasses presents any danger, but I would not drink much of any spirits that have been stored for long periods in lead crystal decanters. There's too much opportunity for the lead to leach into the highly alcoholic liquid.

Wine Spectator once evaluated 21 different lines of wine glasses ranging in price from $4 to $120 per stem. The differences were extraordinary. Riedel showed well in every price range, but others also appealed to us, including glasses from Pottery Barn in the under-$15 price range, Lenox and Tiffany in the $15–$40 range, and Baccarat in the over-$40 range. A good department store will have a wide range of stemware. Use glasses that suit your taste, your budget and your wines.

WHILE EXPENSIVE CRYSTAL IS BEAUTIFUL, REMEMBER THAT LESS EXPENSIVE STEMWARE IS CERTAINLY ACCEPTABLE.

How much to pour into a wine glass

You want enough wine in the glass so you can see the depth and hue of the color clearly when you tilt the glass, enough so it will release the volatile aroma components when the contents are swirled, and enough to give you a good taste. But don't pour so much that the wine spills when swirled. One-third full is a good rule of thumb; in glasses with extremely large bowls, pour no more than five or six ounces.

Caring for glasses

Wine glasses require a slightly different approach from water and juice glasses. Crystal can lose its clarity if it is washed with harsh detergents, and any residue in the glass can affect wine. In particular, any vestige of dishwashing liquid can hinder the formation of bubbles when you pour a Champagne or sparkling wine; it is surprising how anemic a Champagne can look in a not-quite-sparkling glass. Scorching hot water will rinse off soap scum, but unless a glass is greasy from contact with something other than wine and lips I prefer to just wash it in very hot water, sans soap.

As for dishwashers, use one only if it has a gentle setting for crystal and you can be sure the glasses won't clink into each other; never use detergent, which can eventually etch and cloud crystal. I prefer to wash all my crystal by hand. (Remember that the stems of the glasses are fragile. Holding a glass by the stem and twisting the bowl can break the stem, especially when drying. Hold the glass by the bowl.)

Breathing: what it accomplishes, what it does not

Does a wine breathe? Well, no, not literally, but once it has been exposed to air, chemical changes occur. The changes are real, although some wines seem to respond to airing more profoundly than others. Collectively, these changes are known as "breathing."

Opening a bottle and pouring out the wine exposes the wine to its first gulp of air since it was bottled. Ideally, a stoppered bottle should not allow any oxygen to get in or out. A few stray molecules could seep one way or the other, but not enough to affect the wine, if the cork is doing its job right.

Having lived without benefit of oxygen for so long, bottled wine can take a few minutes to reveal what it has. It can seem closed-up at first, only to unfold an amazing range of flavors within 10 or 15 minutes. Off aromas can dissipate with exposure to air. Over the years, these kinds of changes have convinced otherwise sane wine fanciers to build an arcane set of procedures around the simple suggestion of "letting it breathe."

Rather than drive yourself nuts, I recommend keeping it simple. Open a wine and pour it. Enjoy the way it changes in the glass.

Don't just leave it in the bottle

How many times has this happened? A waiter brings the bottle you ordered, opens it and asks, "Should I pour it, or let it breathe?" Then he departs, leaving the full bottle, its cork removed. This is one of the enduring myths of wine. Let's bust it right now and forever. That dime-sized circle of surface area could not absorb enough air to make a dime's worth of difference in the wine even if you left it like that for an hour.

Just go ahead and pour the wine into glasses (or, if necessary, decant it). The act of splashing the wine into the glass oxygenates it. The larger surface area exposes the wine to more air. And removing some of the wine from the bottle exposes a larger surface area in the bottle to air.

Breathing as a predictor of aging

This one always amuses me. Otherwise knowledgeable people believe that if a wine improves significantly in the glass over several hours, or if the last few drops taste better the next day, it means the wine can age well. This makes little sense because those changes are the result of exposure to oxygen. They are, in chemical terms, aerobic reactions. As a wine ages in the bottle, totally different chemical changes occur because of the lack of oxygen. They are anaerobic.

The only connection is that wines made well enough to taste good a day after opening are probably made well enough to age. But you can tell that from tasting them right after opening. You don't need to save any to taste tomorrow.

Bottle variation

There are many reasons why one bottle of the same wine can taste different from the next one. In a young wine, this can result from the wine being bottled from different barrels or vats, from shipping and storage problems, or from an imperfect cork. Older wines almost always vary from one bottle to another. They just evolve differently, especially so with delicate wines such as Burgundy. Hence the aphorism among wine collectors, "there are no great old Burgundies, only great old bottles."

That said, the differences in younger wines are not usually great. Judging by the wines we recheck in the *Wine Spectator* tasting room, the incidence of bad bottles among young wines seems to be around 5% to 8%. About half of that is attributable to cork taint. If you open a second bottle of that wine you loved last week and it seems a little different, it could be bottle variation.

Getting to the right temperature

Most red wines taste best at around 65° to 70° F., a little cooler than the prevailing temperatures in most American rooms. Most white wines do best around 45° to 50° F. Depending on where you keep your wine, you must think ahead to serve wine at the temperature at which it tastes best.

The best way to chill wine is in an ice bucket. Loosely fill the bucket with ice and then—this is really important—add water to cover the ice. It drives me nuts to see wine bottles in restaurants perched on top of ice buckets because the cubes are so tightly packed together the waiter could not get

the bottle buried in the ice. Besides, ice water chills a bottle more efficiently than ice alone because every square millimeter of the bottle is in contact with the source of cold.

And please, waiters: Totally immerse those bottles in the ice and water. Otherwise the bottom of the bottle gets nice and cold while the top few inches end up warm in the first glasses poured.

If there is enough time, an hour or two in the refrigerator will also work. In an emergency, a little chill in the freezer won't hurt a wine any more than immersing it in a water bath with ice—though the latter actually is more effective, because water chills faster than air. Set a timer so the freezer doesn't overdo it, however. You don't want the wine to freeze and push out the cork. Fifteen minutes is usually plenty.

Because Champagne is meant to be served very cold, I keep a bottle or two in the refrigerator all the time, ready for duty. It's a pain to have to ice it down at the last minute, and it's nice to be able to pull out a chilled bottle whenever the mood strikes you.

Red wines left on a warm sideboard in the kitchen can be too warm to enjoy. There's no harm in chilling them just as you would white wines, but for a shorter period, just to cool them off a little. Red wines right out of a temperature-controlled cellar can be too cold, however (see chapter 8). An hour at room temperature usually does the trick.

What to do with the rest of the wine

Inevitably, the question arises of what do whatever remains in the bottle after you have had enough. If you just re-cork the wine and set it on the counter, oxidation will make some wines taste pallid and uninteresting within hours, and most table wines within a day or two.

The easiest option is to re-cork the bottle and put it in the refrigerator, because cold slows down the oxidation process. The opened wine will last a day or two at refrigerator temperatures. You can also buy wine-keeping systems that use inert gases such as nitrogen or argon to displace the air in the bottle. Nitrogen is even available in spray cans for this purpose. Nitrogen is heavier than air, so it sinks over the wine to create a barrier to oxygen. I have kept wines fresh for as long as a week with nitrogen.

A widely available product pumps some of the air from the bottle, creating a partial vacuum. To my taste, wines kept this way are not as fresh-tasting as those kept under simple refrigeration.

More drastic measures are needed to keep a partially empty bottle longer than a few days, however. One neat trick is to store leftover wine in stoppered beer bottles or 375-milliliter wine bottles, filled to the top. The wine itself displaces most of the air and will keep for months, even years, wherever you normally keep your wine. Be sure to label it correctly.

We aim to freeze

I strongly recommend a more unorthodox approach. Put the re-corked bottle in the freezer, where it will keep almost indefinitely. Freezing is not perfect. Wine does lose something when frozen and thawed, mainly tannin and acidity, but the flavors remain 95 percent intact. And you can wait six months to finish that bottle, which you can't do with other methods (unless you save exactly a half bottle or the equivalent in a beer bottle).

And that's the key. You can open other wines without feeling guilty about losing the rest of the first bottle. It will be in the freezer waiting for you.

Corks slide back into bottles best if they go in upside down, so freeze bottles upright to keep the wine from touching the cork. Any mold remaining on the outside of the cork won't affect the wine. Once the wine is frozen solid, you can lay it down.

To thaw the wine, stand it upright at room temperature for several hours. Or microwave the bottle on high until a 1-inch piece of ice remains floating in the wine. The wine will not cook if you stop the oven at that point (about 3 minutes for a half-filled bottle); it will be at cool room temperature. If there is sediment, just decant it. (See page 131).

In restaurants: the tasting ritual

This is maybe the most terrifying moment in wine drinking. The pressure is on. Everyone is watching you take a slurp and decide if the wine is worthy. Sweat beads on your forehead. Your mind swirls as fast as the wine in the glass as you try to pick up any nuances of off character. What if I'm wrong and the wine is horrible? Ack! I can't taste a thing! My tastebuds have shut down. Aaargh!

Time out!

First off, relax. You just want to make sure you got what you ordered by checking the label and giving the wine a quick taste. No waiter hovers over a diner waiting to see if the food is OK, but it's part of the sommelier's code to wait

THE AUTHOR TRIES OUT A NEW ROLE AS SOMMELIER.

until you've tasted the wine to make sure it's OK to pour for the table. In real French restaurants, the sommelier does the tasting. That's why he's wearing that little silver tasting cup, called a tastevin. Here, that burden is shifted to the consumer. That's you. But don't panic.

When the waiter pours, you need only taste for two things, and the most important is temperature. That's easy. Is the wine warm to the taste or so cold you can't taste it? Have that remedied first (see below, "Who cooked/froze my wine?"). The other task is to assess enough of the flavor to know if the wine is really awful. Don't be shy about giving the wine a second sip if the first one seems a little hinky. If you can drink it without wincing, nod to the waiter and let things proceed.

If you're not sure, say so. I have been known to say (especially if I'm reviewing the restaurant), "This doesn't taste quite right," and look up expectantly. That throws the ball back into their court. Ha!

You can always throw a penalty flag on the wine later, should you find a flaw after drinking a few more sips. It happens. It has happened to me. If that hint of earthiness that seemed so charming on first sip now tastes like they fined it with mud, just call the waiter or sommelier, give her the "This doesn't taste quite right" line, and invite her to taste it, too. No sweat.

The cork presentation

At some point after extracting the cork, the waiter will probably hand it to you or set it on the table next to you. There is a good reason for this, but it does not involve smelling it. Look at it to make sure it's not all dry and crumbly, and to see if it has any markings. Many fine wines print the name of the wine and the vintage on the cork. If you ordered Château Gâteau and the cork says Château Profiterole, point it out. (Go ahead and taste the wine anyway. You might like it—but you have no obligation to keep it if you don't.)

The cork can give clues to the wine's storage and condition, but it's not impossible to have a poor cork in a great wine, and tasting the wine itself is really the only way to judge its quality. By the way, I appreciate it if the waiter removes the cork after I accept the wine.

Who cooked/froze my wine?

Serving temperature is one of my biggest bugaboos. I run into this problem all over the world. I have a very direct approach. I ask for an ice bucket if the wine is too warm (and the bucket must be deep enough to submerge all of the wine in ice and water, or it cools unevenly). For wine already poured, I swirl an ice cube in the glass for a few seconds, then remove it with a spoon or fork. This often scandalizes servers (and sometimes my dining partners) but it does not dilute the wine perceptibly, and I can now enjoy it.

If a wine is served too cold, first get rid of the ice bucket. Ask the waiter to serve small portions, and cup the glass in your hands so the heat of your body warms the wine. (At home, I have been known to microwave a glass of wine for 3-4 seconds to take the chill off it.)

Restaurant wine prices and practices

Every restaurant has its own formula for pricing wine. Some want to encourage their customers to order wine by keeping prices low. Others with an eye on the bottom line believe they must charge enough for wine to be a profit center. That's why one restaurant might price a given wine at $40 and another charge $75. It's tempting to blame greed, but the reasons are a little more complicated than that.

Some restaurants invest in expensive crystal glasses (which also break more readily than bar glass), build up several years' wine inventory (which ties up money but gives you more choices) and spend time and money training staff to do things right. They deserve to charge a little more, but surprisingly, their prices often fall into the middle range. The restaurants that charge the most usually have a high-priced menu to go along with their luxe wine list.

Within this wide range of pricing philosophies, the closest thing to an industry standard markup is $2^{1}/_{2}$ or 3 times the price the restaurant paid. A wine that wholesales for $10 a bottle goes for $15 in a retail shop and $20 to $30 in a typical restaurant. (Restaurants usually take a higher markup on food costs, by the way, but they also have to apply more labor to food.)

Smart restaurateurs take a smaller percentage markup on higher-priced wines. Smart customers know that the lowest-priced wines on a restaurant wine list are not the best bargains. The best buys are usually in the mid-to-high range. Wines that have been in the cellar for a few years can represent the best values of all if the restaurant has resisted raising the prices over the years.

BYOB and corkage fees

What if you want to bring your own wine to a restaurant? In most states, you can bring your own bottle (BYOB). For opening it and letting you use their glasses, most restaurants will charge a corkage fee. (My friend Dan wishes that restaurants with great wine lists and lousy food would let him bring a box lunch and charge him "forkage". But I digress.)

Some snotty restaurants refuse to let customers bring wine, but most wine-friendly restaurants won't mind if you follow a few common courtesies.

1. Don't bring a wine that the restaurant sells. Saving a few bucks this way is cheap and insulting. Instead, choose wines from your own cellar that you have been saving for a special occasion.

2. When you make the reservation, tell the host that you want to bring in a special bottle (or bottles), and make sure there are no objections. The host should tell you at this time of any corkage fees.

3. At dinner, offer a glass of your wine to the sommelier, chef or owner. This often encourages better food and service. Thus lubricated, some sommeliers even forget the corkage fee.

Wines by the glass

The days are gone when wine by the glass was always cheap plonk. Better restaurants today pride themselves in offering a wide range of good wines by the glass at fair prices. For customers like us, good wines by the glass allow the one person at a table of six having venison to drink a nice red when everyone else is having fish and white wine.

A restaurant should not keep an open wine for more than two nights, unless an inert gas wine-keeping system such as a Cruvinet protects it against oxidation. If you think a wine has been open too long and no longer delivers the quality it should, don't hesitate to ask for a glass from a fresh bottle.

Tipping

I almost always tip 20 percent on my restaurant bills. If the service is good or better, and if the wine is a moderately priced bottle, I'll just base the tip on the total check. In most restaurants today, tips are pooled and then divided up by the staff, anyway. I don't believe it's necessary to include whopping wine bills in the calculation. If a sommelier has been particularly helpful, I might tip him or her directly ($10 or $20 per bottle), then base the waiter's tip on the rest of the bill.

Of course, generosity is uniformly appreciated and may even help improve your dining experience the next time you're in the restaurant.

The Essence

Wine bottles come in various shapes, dictated by tradition and sometimes by marketing or packaging considerations. Stoppers traditionally are made from cork, which seals well but can taint a wine if the cork is moldy. Plastic stoppers made to look and feel like cork are gaining credibility, but no one knows if they can keep wine in good shape as long as real cork can.

To get into a bottle, the best devices are waiter's corkscrews or more modern versions such as those patented by Screwpull.

Older wines need to be handled carefully. The older the wine, the greater the risk that the bottle might be disappointing. Whenever you serve an older wine, have extra bottles ready to open (even of another wine, if necessary) in case the first one fails to meet expectations. Older wines often form a sediment inside the bottle over time. (See page 131 for decanting techniques.)

CHAPTER SEVEN

How to Get into a Wine Bottle

For something that's been popular for as long as wine, it sure comes in an inconvenient package. The cork stopper, a relic of early glass blowing, is the major culprit. It requires a special tool to pull it out. For the uninitiated, the most intimidating aspect of wine might very well be the simple act of opening a bottle. To take the sting out of the subject, let's see how a wine bottle is constructed and learn the trick to getting the cork out of it.

Anatomy of a wine bottle

Wine bottles vary in shape, depending on regional, cultural and marketing considerations. A standard wine bottle holds 750 milliliters, or 25.4 ounces. The basic shapes (see below) include a straight-shouldered type (usually called a Bordeaux bottle), a slope-shouldered type (Burgundy bottle), an elongated type (hock bottle, used for German and

THE BASIC WINE BOTTLE STYLES: 1. BORDEAUX 2. BURGUNDY 3. ELONGATED OR HOCK 4. CHAMPAGNE 5. PORT (WITH A WAX-DIPPED STOPPER).

German-style wines) and an extra-heavy slope-shouldered bottle designed for Champagne and sparkling wine. Recently, bottle designers have been manipulating these basic shapes into some interesting proprietary packages, as well.

Most wine bottles also have an indentation in the bottom called the punt. This bump in the bottom strengthens the structure of the container, which was necessary in the days of handblown bottles that varied significantly in thickness. These days, it's more for show—to maintain a traditional look. Champagne bottles, which must withstand extra pressure, have especially deep punts, as do the most expensive wines. The punt also is a convenient place to position your thumb if you hold the bottle from the bottom to pour. (You might notice a white paint mark on the bottom edge of some bottles, usually Champagne and Port. On Champagne, the white mark helps keep track of how far the bottle was rotated when it was being hand-riddled. On Port bottles, it indicates which side was up when the unlabeled bottles were resting untouched so as not to disturb the sediment forming in them.)

To close the bottle, a cork is pushed in flush with the end of the bottle's neck. The lip is protected with a capsule that once was made of lead, but is now most often made of plastic or aluminum foil. The stoppered ends of Port bottles are often dipped in melted wax. Some bottles are designed with decorative lips and do away with the foil altogether; a small dollop of wax or a clear plastic sheath protects the exposed surface of the cork.

Champagne and sparkling wine corks stick out from the bottle top, creating the familiar mushroom shape. Actually, the cork is not mushroom shaped before it goes into the bottle. It's an extra-wide cylindrical shape. A clamp squeezes the portion of the cork that fits into the bottle. Before it can spring back, it is inserted, affixed with a wire cage, and covered with foil to keep it clean.

Corks

Corks are made from the bark of a cork oak tree, which is peeled away in big sheets. The flexible bark is shot through with little air sacs, like a wooden sponge. When the cork is cut into its familiar cylindrical shape, these form tiny suction cups on the surface, which adhere to the inside of the bottle's neck, making a perfect seal.

For the most part, corks work great, but they have their problems. Sometimes the seal is incomplete and the wine leaks. Corks can also harbor a mold that spoils the wine with something called cork taint, which smells like rotting newspapers. A wine suffering from this malady is said to be "corky" or "corked." (I find the term "corky" less confusing than "corked"; after all, aren't most wine bottles corked?)

Stoppers made from various forms of plastic designed to behave like natural cork are being used more and more often. They eliminate the problem of cork taint, but so far the jury is out on how artificial corks will affect wine during long storage. A new development announced in 1999 involves applying microwave radiation to natural corks

SYNTHETIC CORKS HAVE BECOME INCREASINGLY POPULAR IN RECENT YEARS.

before shipping, a procedure that seems effective in killing the mold. No wines were bottled with microwave-treated corks prior to 2000.

Getting into the bottle

Part 1: Table wine

Most corkscrews, even the most elaborate, work on the same basic principle. A plain corkscrew consists of a metal helix (called a worm) attached to a handle. You twist the worm through the center of the cork and use brute strength to yank the cork out, holding the bottle steady with one hand or your knees. As the cork emerges, it comes out faster and faster, so take care not to splash or spill.

SUCCESSFUL USE OF THE PLAIN CORKSCREW REQUIRES A GOOD DEAL OF STRENGTH.

The waiter's corkscrew adds leverage to the basic corkscrew. It is the most widely used tool for removing corks from wine bottles. Here's how to use it.

THE WAITER'S CORKSCREW.

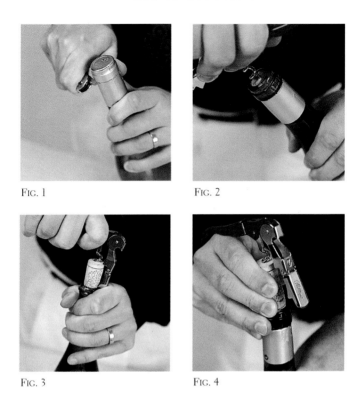

Fig. 1   Fig. 2

Fig. 3   Fig. 4

Fig. 1. Use the knife to cut away the capsule just below the flange. (Or, less formally, just pull off the whole capsule.)

Fig. 2. Open the corkscrew at a 90° angle and the lever mechanism as far as it will go. Pierce the top of the cork with the sharp point of the corkscrew. Continue to twist the screw right through the center of the cork.

Fig 3. Rock the handle back so the lever mechanism rests on the lip and hold the mechanism steady to keep it from slipping. Lift the handle straight up, slowly at first, until the cork comes out.

Fig. 4. If the cork is very long, you may need to pull it the rest of the way. It should come out easily.

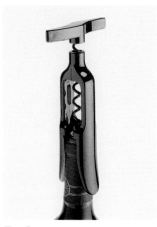

THE SCREWPULL.   THE SCREWPULL LEVER MODEL.

Among dozens of different corkscrew designs, a few work especially well. A patented product, Screwpull, uses an extra-long Teflon-coated worm mounted inside a clothespin-like frame that fits over the bottle's lip. The user just keeps twisting the screw while the cork rides up the worm

THE TWO-PRONGED CORK EXTRACTOR, CALLED AN AH-SO

and right out of the bottle. If you must open a lot of bottles, get the waiter's Screwpull, which is easier on the hand and wrist muscles because the user rotates the screw with a stirring motion instead of twisting. Easiest of all, Screwpull's elaborate Lever model clamps onto a bottle and removes the cork with a single thrust of the lever.

One useful device that does not use the traditional metal helix is the two-pronged cork extractor named Ah-So. It consists of two metal strips—curved crosswise to follow the contour of a wine cork—

attached to a handle. The user slides the metal strips vertically between the cork and the glass with a gentle rocking motion; then the cork comes out when you make a twisting motion, like unscrewing a light bulb. This device works especially well on old, crumbly corks.

Part 2: Sparkling wine

Champagne and sparkling wine come in bottles with a distinctive protruding cork held in place with a wire cage. Because the wine inside is under pressure, be careful when opening these bottles. Always keep a hand on the cork. If the cork is loose, it can rocket out of the bottle, ricochet off a wall or ceiling and injure someone.

Here is my fail-safe procedure:

Fig. 5 Remove the foil.

Fig. 6. Resting your hand on top of the cork to keep it from shooting out, untwist the cage-like closure so it is free of the bottle's lip.

Fig. 5

Fig. 7 Without removing the cage, grasp the cork and with the other hand lift the bottle, holding it at about a 45° angle. (Holding the bottle at an angle increases the surface area of wine inside the bottle and minimizes foaming.) Gently twist the bottle (not the cork). As it loosens, you should feel the pressure of gas in the wine pushing the cork out of the bottle.

Fig. 6

Fig. 7

Fig. 8. Keep a grip on the cork as it slides out of the bottle. You don't want to hear a loud pop, just a quiet little exhalation of carbon dioxide from the bottle. Have a glass ready to pour the wine into if it starts to foam too much.

Fɪɢ. 8

Part 3: Port and the like

Port bottles, and other bottles similarly sealed with wax, can be a real mess to open. Trying to cut the wax only scatters shards of it all over the place. The secret, surprisingly, is heat. Light a candle and hold the tip of the bottle over it to soften the wax. It then should cut away smoothly.

Brave souls may want to try using a pair of port tongs. These are heated in the fireplace, then clamped onto the neck of the bottle just below the lip. The red-hot tongs go right through the wax and into the glass itself. A wet cloth applied to the spot after the tongs are removed makes a clean break in the glass where the tongs heated it. (Not recommended for beginners.)

In a pinch, you can always take the bottle out back and chip away where the wax shards won't bother anyone.

Dealing with older wines

Remember that older red wines often have sediment which forms in the bottle as the wine ages. You can treat these bottles gently, keeping them as close to horizontal as possible and carrying them gingerly from rack to table. Or you can stand them up several hours to a day in advance so the sediment settles to the bottom. (I have friends who even shake up the bottle before standing it up, on the theory that this loosens any sediment that might otherwise stick to the side of the bottle.)

Have a two-pronged cork extractor ready to deal with brittle, crumbly or stuck corks. If the cork gets pushed into the wine, there is a tool with three thin wire hooks that can capture the cork. Or, just hold the cork inside the bottle with a chopstick while decanting the wine.

Be sure to wipe the top of the bottle with a damp cloth before extracting the cork and again before pouring to remove any fungus that might have formed under the foil. (It won't harm you, but it might taint the flavor.)

With any older wine, always have a backup bottle ready, just in case the bottle turns out to be bad or disappointing. Even in the best cellars, wines can be corky or just go over the hill and lose their charm. At some dinner parties, I have been known to fetch three or four replacements until we found one we wanted to keep drinking.

THE CORK LIFT IS A HANDY TOOL FOR CAPTURING A CORK THAT HAS FALLEN INTO THE WINE.

The d-word: decanting

After the removal of the cork, the second most intimidating thing about wine is decanting it. Fancy restaurants make it into a ritual, but it need not be. Decanting simply separates any sediment from the clear wine. Generally, I decant only if the wine is old enough to have sediment in the bottle. Decanting also aerates the wine, so it is worth decanting if experience has shown that a particular wine improves with exposure to air.

POSITIONING A LIGHT SOURCE BENEATH THE NECK OF THE BOTTLE YOU ARE
DECANTING WILL HELP YOU SEE THE TINY WISPS OF SEDIMENT SNEAKING
INTO IT.

Another reason for decanting is to put the wine into a
neutral container if you don't want to reveal the bottle, as
at a blind-tasting party. Or, perhaps you just want to show
off a lovely decanter.

Decanting is a pretty basic process. You need a clean
container. It can be a decanter or a water jug. You also
need a light source (a candle, flashlight, or perhaps one of
those clip-on reading lights) positioned to shine up through
the neck of the bottle as you slowly, gently (so as not to
shake up the gunk) start pouring the wine into the clean
container. When you start to see wisps of sediment (Fig. 9)
sneak into the neck of the bottle, stop pouring. Serve from
the decanter, or rinse out the wine bottle and pour the wine

back into it through a funnel (a useful tactic when bringing older wines to restaurants).

Either decant the wine just before serving, or, if you don't want to perform for your guests, decant the wine before they arrive, rinse out the bottle, pour the wine back in, and replace the cork. This minimizes the wine's exposure to air until you want it exposed—in the glass.

FIG. 9

The Essence

Buy by the case, or at least in multiple bottles, which postpones the inevitable pain of drinking the last bottle and wishing you had more.

To determine how big your cellar should be, a good rule of thumb is to take the number of bottles you expect to drink from your storage per year and multiply by 10. This provides enough for you to drink some wines within five years and to age others for 15 or more.

If you have the space, you can build your own storage area that will keep the temperature steady at around 55°F. To avoid a construction project, you can buy stand-alone storage units, or rent space from a wine shop or temperature-controlled warehouse.

Develop a system to keep track of your wine, such as a card file, cellar book or computer database. Once a collection starts to grow, it's too easy to misplace a bottle.

If you decide to purchase wine as a financial investment, buy wine that you'll enjoy drinking. If you can't sell it later at a profit, you can always drink it.

CHAPTER EIGHT

Keeping Wine: Hows and Whys

Sooner or later, everyone who drinks wine collects a few bottles to put away for the future, buying it when it is most available and affordable. Before you know it, you have a cellar—not literally a basement, but a supply of ready-to-drink wines for dinner.

Some wines take longer than others to reach that ready stage, but the principle is the same whether you plan to hold wine for three years or 30. Chances are, you will amass more red wine than white. The arithmetic is simple. Red wines generally take longer to get where you want them, so you must stockpile more years of red wines before you get around to drinking them.

Though you might have a particular fascination with certain wines, try to acquire more than just your favorite Bordeaux and Cabernet Sauvignon (or Rhône or Brunello or Burgundy or Pinot Noir). Keep things in balance. If your cellar covers various points in the style spectrum, you can readily serve big reds with hearty dishes and elegant wines with lighter dishes. The moment of triumph comes when you dust off a 25- or 30-year-old bottle for a special occasion, pull the cork and know that the glorious liquid being shared around the table came from your own collection.

Getting started

Fortunately, it doesn't take big money to start a respectable wine cellar. The following strategy suggests which wines to buy, how much to buy, how much to spend, and how to build a collection that will reflect your own personality and preferences.

First rule: Only buy wines you expect to drink. Even if at some point you decide to buy wine as a financial investment, thinking of what they will be worth 10, 15 or 20 years down the road, you can always drink the profits if the market goes south. If your cellar is primarily a taste investment, designed to provide mature wine to drink yourself and with friends, you will be ahead of the game.

Buy by the case

Either way, most everyone who has done this for a while agrees that it's best to buy by the case, or at least multiple bottles. For investors, full cases are worth more than single bottles. For drinkers, nothing is more bittersweet than to consume your only bottle of a great wine knowing that it might be even better in two, five or 10 years. With a full case you can open several bottles along the way and know exactly how the wine is developing.

Many of us start a wine collection by accumulating single bottles of special wines on trips to wine country or visits to good wine shops. You might not think you can afford to buy more than a bottle or two at a time, but at the moment of truth, when the wine touches the lips, you will wish you had. Each bottle will be a memorable experience, but if it is your only bottle it will be unrepeatable.

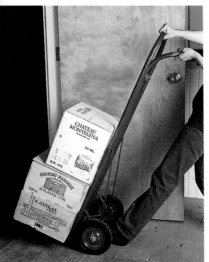

Better to have enough to enjoy the wine throughout its evolution.

More to the point, having at least several bottles of a given wine takes some pressure off the perennial when-to-drink-it quandary. The only thing worse than opening a prized bottle only to find that it has not progressed to the ready-and-willing stage is to discover that you waited too long.

Better to drink a wine on the way up, knowing that more bottles await.

Buying wine for children and anniversaries

The idea of "putting down" some wine that is vintage-dated with the birth year of a newborn sounds like a good idea, but it is fraught with pitfalls. First of all, finding a wine that will still be good 20 to 30 years down the road is a tricky enough proposition. Most French and California reds are best at seven to 15 years of age. Whether a wine will last beyond that is a roll of the dice, and will only happen in great vintages—and no one can predict with precision what a given vintage will be like.

Trying to find a wine that is modestly priced makes the problem harder, since lower-priced wines are generally not meant for aging. Having said that, I would suggest you keep your eyes open for a sweet wine, such as late-harvest Riesling or Sémillon. A sweet wine is more likely to age longer than a red wine would, and your young charge is more likely to enjoy it in his or her 20s.

Perhaps a better plan is to select a wine for you to drink on the anniversaries of your child's or grand-child's birth over the next five to 20 years, exactly as you would for a wedding anniversary or other adult-oriented remembrance.

MANY WEALTHY COLLECTORS HAVE EXTRAORDINARY PRIVATE CELLARS BUILT IN THEIR HOMES TO HOUSE AND DISPLAY THEIR VAST HOLDINGS.

A cellar plan

Wine differs from other collectibles in that its eventual purpose is to be consumed completely. Every wine has an expected lifetime, and any cellar plan must account for depletions, replacing the drunk-up bottles with something else. A working cellar creates a flow of good wine, some of which will be ready to drink over the next few years, while another portion will require more time. Wines that need to age the longest generally cost more than those that need only a few years.

(Because most modestly priced wines are best within a year of purchase, they frankly need no cellaring, just a place to store them for a few months until you use them up. They are not part of a cellar plan, which focuses on wines that reveal their splendors over time.)

• For about $2,000 to $3,000 you should be able to start with 12 to 15 cases (144 to 180 bottles) of wines that are best consumed within three to five years. Average price per bottle: $15 to $20.

EPARGNEZ L'EAU
BUVEZ DU VIN

• For about $10,000 you can add about 25 cases of wines that *need* at least three to five years to be at their best and should continue to be enjoyable for five to 10 years beyond that. Thus, you can drink the contents of the first cellar while waiting for this cellar to mature. Average price per bottle: $30 to $40.

• Big spenders can invest further in high-profile, sure-thing, long-term investments, big-ticket wines you can expect to appreciate in quality and value over many years. You can also buy mature wines from better retailers or at auction.

In each category, divide your investment among these general types of wine that can repay time in the cellar:
- claret-style reds (Bordeaux and California Cabernet);
- big reds (such as Rhône, Shiraz and Zinfandel);
- elegant reds (such as Burgundy, Pinot Noir, Merlot and Rioja)
- ageable whites (such as Burgundy, Chardonnay and German/Alsace wines);
- sweet wines (such as Sauternes, late harvest and Port).

What to buy

At any given time, much depends on the quality of the most recent vintages. The Bordeaux vintages 1994, 1995 and 1996 all produced ageworthy wines, for example. The previous three produced mostly wines not worth cellaring—unless you're so fascinated by Bordeaux that you want every vintage, for better or worse. Buyers who were ignoring Bordeaux woke up and paid attention as the 1994s, 1995s and 1996s arrived.

If the market is filled with ageable California Cabernet, and you like Cabernet, make it a high priority. When the currently available vintage of Italian Brunello di Montalcino gets high marks, pounce on the wines as soon as you can if you want them. If you like Burgundy and the available vintage is mediocre, bide your time, waiting for better wines.

What is worth cellaring

Keep in mind that ageable wine is a relatively rare commodity. Start with the assumption that most of the world's wine is meant to be consumed before the next vintage. Even those wines that benefit from three to five years' aging are not meant to go on for much longer. And among the relatively small number of wines that will actually improve with cellaring, the sad fact is that most of them are made in tiny quantities. All great *grand cru* Burgundy, red and

white; most Côte-Rôtie, Hermitage, Barolo, Barbaresco and Brunello; and even much California Cabernet Sauvignon falls into that category.

What that means for serious collectors is that every vintage is a new treasure hunt. Knowing which wines are the best is only the beginning. Finding them requires some perseverance.

One reason most wine collectors focus on Bordeaux is that the châteaus produce plenty of wine. Most of the top ones make at least 15,000 cases each vintage, often as many as 35,000 cases. But Domaine de la Romanée-Conti La Tâche (which qualifies as a blue-chip Burgundy for the cellar) produces only 1,000 cases in a bumper vintage, Gaja Barbaresco Sorì Tildìn about the same—and they are among the larger vineyards in their regions.

Although the same is true for some of the hottest names in California, there are plenty of big-volume California Cabernet Sauvignons and Chardonnays, including some of the state's most famous—not to mention Bordeaux, Australian Shiraz, Chianti, Ribera del Duero, and a host of lesser-known wines also worthy of cellaring.

How much space?

Although lavish wine cellars with beautifully designed cedar racks are lovely to have, all you really need is a cool, dark place to put your bottles until you are ready to drink them. How much space depends on how much wine. How much wine depends on how often you plan to make withdrawals from the cellar. Someone who has dinner parties several times a week obviously will use more wine—and need more space to store it—than someone who has two or four friends over for dinner twice a month.

To figure out how much space you need, first figure out how many bottles to store. Estimate how much wine you might use per year and multiply by 10. That allows for a supply of wines to be used up in five years, and another five years' supply of long-term wines to use over the next five. (One assumes, of course, that these wines would be replaced with later vintages as they are consumed. Also, assume that everyday wines and current-vintage white wines and Champagnes for dinner parties are not part of this equation.)

Example 1. Adam and Agatha make dinners for four once a month and bring a bottle to dinner out maybe once a week. They can figure on using six bottles a month from the cellar (not counting wines for current drinking). That's six cases a year. They will need space for 30 cases each of short-term and long-term wines, a total of 60 cases.

Example 2. Bill and Betty entertain twice a month and bring a bottle to dinner out twice a week. That's about a case of wine a month, 12 cases per year. They will need space for at least 120 cases.

Example 3. Carl and Cathy give dinner parties for eight every week and go out to eat often, bringing along wine from the cellar each time. They might go through 36 cases a year. They will need space for 360 cases.

Storage intelligence

You can start a wine collection without actually building a cellar. Use closets and corners around the house, avoiding exterior walls. Eventually, you may want to set aside a designated space for wine storage. Think of it as a slightly more elaborate pantry. Or you might want to rent space in a commercial facility. Some basic considerations:

Temperature. The single most important consideration is to keep the wine cool. Wine does best at 55-60° F, which happens to be the temperature of an underground cellar. Most homes or apartments are at 68-72° F, which will do for a year or two.

Temperature swings. Any location that is not underground or artificially cooled gets warmer during the day and cools off at night. It also gets warmer in the summer, colder in the winter. These temperature swings can accelerate wine's aging process. One way to moderate these temperature fluctuations is to pack the bottles tightly. According to the principle of thermal inertia, a large mass of liquid takes longer to warm up (and to cool down) than a smaller mass does. Packing the bottles close together creates a large liquid mass.

Put a thermometer in a bottle. Insert a thermometer with a long spike (like a meat thermometer) through the cork of a cheap bottle of wine. This bottle, placed amidst the rest of your wine, accurately reads the temperature of the wine in your cellar. A thermometer on the wall only measures the air around it.

Humidity. Moist cellars keep corks from drying out, but they can encourage mold. You should see some of the cellars in France. The walls are covered with fur. It's not harmful, but inevitably, some of the mold gets trapped under the capsule when the wine is bottled there, and grows under the closed capsule. For that reason, Old World wineries cellar the bottles without capsules. Most of us put up with the mold on the lip and make sure to wipe it off before pouring. Don't remove the capsules if you plan to resell the wine. A capsule-less wine loses some of its resale value, even though the cork will be in better shape.

Light. Bottles meant to age are tinted dark green, sometimes brown, to protect the wine from light. Don't be paranoid, however. It's OK to turn on the bulb when you visit your cellar. Just don't leave it on when you're not there.

Vibration. It stirs up the sediment. Don't keep wine next to the washing machine or dryer.

Horizontal position. Wine likes to lie down comfortably and keep its cork wet. Resist the temptation to display prize wines upright.

OOPS LIST
or
OH NO! WHAT'S WRONG WITH MY WINE?

Don't panic if you extract a bottle from your cellar and find something amiss. Often, it's not as bad as it looks. Here are some of the things that can happen:

BAD

Tastes like wet newspapers. That's the classic taste of corkiness. A mold that lives in a small percentage of corks can infect the wine. In small doses it makes the wine taste like it has no flavor. In larger concentrations, it tastes kind of earthy. Full-blown corkiness tastes awful. There is no way to identify a corky bottle without tasting the wine. Corky wine is not harmful, it just tastes bad.

Did somebody cook the wine? If it tastes cooked, it was probably exposed to heat somewhere along the way. It doesn't take much. A couple of days of 90° F temperatures can affect some delicate wines. Chances are, whatever caused the problem happened before you even got the wine. Shipping companies that do not protect wine in transit are usually at fault. They ship wine in midsummer via the Panama Canal or through the Midwest without adequate cooling systems. They leave pallets of wine on the docks in New Jersey or Texas for days on end. Fie on them.

Tastes flat, stale. The bane of aging wine. It was probably left in the cellar too long, and it's past its prime. The wine just wasn't up to such a long aging time. Alternatively, it could be a mild case of corkiness.

Floods, earthquakes and other real disasters. A good friend opened his cellar door one day to find three feet of water. Labels floated like little rafts on the surface. Fortunately, cork makes a good enough seal that none of the wine was affected. But how to tell which unlabeled bottle was which? Most European vintners stamp the cork with the winery name and the vintage, which helps. It's not a perfect solution. If you have two or three single-vineyard wines from one winery, you're out of luck identifying them. And you can't even see the cork without removing the capsule. Earthquakes at least leave the labels intact if they don't shatter the bottles. If you live in earthquake country, take special pains to anchor wine racks to the wall studs.

NOT SO BAD

Corroded capsules, mold on the outside of the cork. In the United States, bottles are usually filled, labeled and fitted with capsules in one operation, then stored in boxes prior to shipping. In Europe, unlabeled bottles are usually stored in dank cellars until they are ready to ship, whereupon the bottles are wiped off, labeled and fitted with a capsule to cover the exposed end of the cork. This procedure often traps some molds and bacteria, which are in the cellar's air, under the capsule. Although they can make the capsule look unsightly, fortunately cork makes a good enough seal that they seldom affect the wine inside.

Leakers. Wine leaks through the cork for several reasons. The bottle could have been exposed to high temperatures, which expand the wine and force it through any tiny gaps between the cork and bottle. If the cork made less than a perfect seal, some wine could leak through. It might have been caused by overfilling at the winery. I have had some great wines from bottles that had leaked through the cork. Fortunately, it is a one-way passage—liquid comes out, but no air gets in—so as long as the cork is sound, you're OK. If this is a recently purchased wine you are planning to keep for several years, phone the retailer and describe the situation. If the retailer can assure you that the bottle was properly handled, you can be confident that the weeping is not a big problem.

Wine looks hazy. Wine throws a sediment as the coloring matter and other solids in the wine precipitate out during the aging process. The sediment settles within a day or so. (If the haze does not disappear, chemical changes in the wine may have ruined it.) Stand the bottle up the day before uncorking it and decanting the clear wine off the sediment (see "Decanting," page 131).

Tiny crystals are visible. Natural acids in wine crystallize at low temperatures. If conditions in the winery get cold enough, these tartrate crystals form before bottling, and are removed. Many wineries do this intentionally. (Wineries collect these crystals from the barrels and vats and sell them to makers of baking powder, in which tartrate is a key ingredient.) If not, the first time you put the bottle in the refrigerator, voila! Crystals. They're harmless. Just decant the wine.

Racks and boxes

Wine racks come in two basic forms. The classic wine cellar divides space into large diamond shapes, each holding 12 to 24 bottles (see photo below, top). The other has a cubbyhole for each bottle of wine (photo below, bottom). The classic design crams more wine into available space. The other allows better access to each bottle.

If you have a suitable basement wall and you're handy enough, you can build an inexpensive wine rack using 2-

by-6-inch lumber and sheets of fence wire (see illustration). The 4-inch openings in fence wire are perfect for classic wine bottles. Build a frame with the 2-by-6-inch lumber, supporting it with 1-by-6 boards every 3 feet or so, and staple fence wire over both faces. Use 4-by-4-inch fencing on the front side and 2-by-4-inch fencing on the back. A standard wine bottle goes in neck first. Its neck rests on the 2-by-4-inch fencing. The labels are visible from the front. (The only drawback of this design is that a growing number of wineries these days are using extra-wide bottles that won't fit in the 4-inch-wide space.)

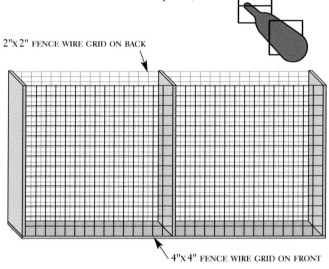

2"x 2" FENCE WIRE GRID ON BACK

4"x 4" FENCE WIRE GRID ON FRONT

How to store a wine collection without resorting to a construction project

If you have a collection of high-quality wines that you want to be sure to keep in top condition, and building a cellar in your home is out of the question, then your two best options for storage are these:

1. Buy a self-contained, temperature-controlled wine storage unit, such as those offered by companies that advertise in the classified ad section of *Wine Spectator*. Such a

A TEMPERATURE-CONTROLLED STORAGE UNIT IS AN IDEAL CHOICE FOR THOSE WITH TOO LITTLE SPACE TO BUILD THEIR OWN CELLAR.

unit is a big investment, but it's an instant solution to the storage problem as long as you have the space for it.

2. Rent space for your collection in a temperature-controlled cellar or warehouse. Many wine merchants provide this service. Check the Yellow Pages or call local retailers. Rates are typically about $2 per month per case. The big disadvantage is that you can usually get your hands on your bottles only during business hours, so you're out of luck if you are in the middle of a dinner party and need an extra bottle of Burgundy.

An old refrigerator is not ideal for wine storage. The thermostat cannot be set high enough to be ideal for wine, and the dehumidifier keeps the environment too dry.

TASTING NOTES

Date of entry _____ Name of wine _____
Occasion or place tasted _____
Price _____ Vintage year _____
Vintner / Producer _____
Country / State / Region _____
Comments and overall quality _____

WINE CELLAR RECORD

Wine _____ Date _____
Purchased from _____ Price _____
Vintner _____
Appellation _____ Vintage _____
Cellar location _____ Original quantity _____
       Date used _____ No. used _____
       Balance _____
Comments/Tasting notes _____

Wine _____ Date _____
Purchased from _____ Price _____
Vintner _____
Appellation _____ Vintage _____
Cellar location _____ Original quantity _____
       Date used _____ No. used _____
       Balance _____
Comments/Tasting notes _____

Wine _____ Date _____
Purchased from _____ Price _____
Vintner _____
Appellation _____ Vintage _____
Cellar location _____ Original quantity _____
       Date used _____ No. used _____
       Balance _____
Comments/Tasting notes _____

Wine _____ Date _____
Purchased from _____ Price _____
Vintner _____
Appellation _____ Vintage _____
Cellar location _____ Original quantity _____
       Date used _____ No. used _____
       Balance _____
Comments/Tasting notes _____

36

Label

A CELLAR BOOK FROM
LETT'S OF LONDON.

Keeping track of your wine

As you add to and subtract from a wine cellar, it can become a motley hodgepodge. Finding a particular bottle when you want it is one good reason to keep some sort of written inventory. If your collection has appreciated significantly in value, it's important for insurance purposes to know how much. And finally, once you open a bottle, it's a good idea to keep a written record of how much you liked it, even if it's just a plus sign for yes and a minus sign for no. That helps narrow the choices next time.

You don't need a cellar book, but most people with wine

cellars like to have some sort of record of at least their big-ticket wines. You can use a fancy bound book with grapevine graphics and places to paste labels, available at your bookstore or wine shop, or a simple loose-leaf notebook.

Computer software

Plenty of computer programs promise to help organize your wines. Some are contained within more elaborate wine software, such as that found on CD-ROMs. Others are designed specifically for wine cellars. Computer software allows you to keep an up-to-date listing of what you have, and easily search it for a given wine. If you're computer-savvy, use a standard database program to set up at least the following fields:

> Winery name/Producer
> Wine type or primary grape variety
> Color
> Region
> Appellation
> Special designation (such as "reserve" or
>   single-vineyard name)
> Vintage
> Number of bottles
> Storage location
> Notes

A PORTION OF A SAMPLE DATABASE RECORD.

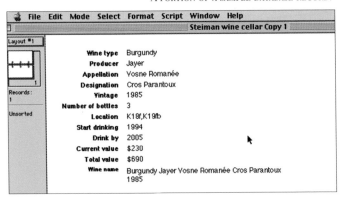

Under "color," the options can include red, white, rosé, sparkling and sweet. The "region" field allows you to sort all the appellation Meursaults and Puligny-Montrachets into the same region group, Burgundy. The "storage location" is a way to find the actual bottle, making it unnecessary to keep them in any special order in the actual cellar, if you don't want to.

Possible additional fields include:

Start drinking (year)
Drink by (year)
Purchase price
Current value
Total value

"Total value" is a calculation of the number of bottles times current value.

The value of a wine collection

Once you start to acquire a significant amount of wine, check whether your current homeowner's insurance covers any loss. Fire, flood or earthquake can destroy a collection in a heartbeat.

You'll probably need to know how much your wine is worth. Information on current values is available from the wine database on *Wine Spectator's* Web site (www. winespectator.com) and from *Wine Spectator's Ultimate Guide to Buying Wine*, updated regularly. Major auction houses are also good sources of current prices for blue-chip wines. You can compile this information yourself, or, if you have a large collection, hire a consultant recommended by an auction house or a respectable retailer to do it for you. Update the prices periodically.

Moving a wine cellar

Approach a pending move by weeding out as much wine as you can before packing up your cellar. Then weed again. Do you really want to schlep that 1987 Chianti across town, let alone across country? The less you move the better.

Moving your wines yourself is probably safer than packing them with the rest of your goods in a moving truck, because you control their exposure to heat. Though wine will probably survive a day or two on the highway at relatively high temperatures, no good comes from it sitting in a moving van parked on some baking tarmac. Upon arrival, unpack your wine immediately into a cool environment, and give the bottles a few weeks to rest after the trip.

Drinkers vs. investors

There are two ways to earn money investing in wine. The safest route is to buy blue-chip wines with a long pedigree. Alas, the wine world has discovered these pedigrees, and driven up the prices on the bottles that have them. This is great news for those who bought before the most recent boom. Their investment has appreciated faster than an Internet IPO. To buy blue-chip wines today, however, requires a substantially greater investment up front than it used to.

In concrete terms, Château Latour 1982 sold for $55 a bottle in 1985, when it was first released. In 1998 it was worth more than $550. To make a comparable killing on a Château Latour 1995 priced at $200 on release in 1998, you must believe that in 2010 it will cost $2,000. That's per bottle.

Savvy collectors look for wines that are less familiar now (and therefore less costly), but will be in great demand later when the rest of the world discovers them. If a winery's future performance makes it a star, the value of its early wines will skyrocket. Those who bought the first vintage of cult favorite Screaming Eagle Cabernet Sauvignon could sell all they have at a 1,000 percent profit—if they were not so intent upon drinking what they bought.

Digging up the most likely candidates among the long list of relative unknowns requires more research, but less financial investment, than buying blue-chip wines. Fortunately, the research is fun, and the more tasting involved the better.

The difference between drinkers and investors is really a matter of style. Drinkers tend to buy personal favorites while investors tend to go for the big names. Drinkers would argue that a cellar filled with blue-chip wines would be like having a music collection consisting of top-selling recordings and nothing by those quirky, less popular musicians you love so much.

One investment strategy

A successful wine collector in Texas came up with a novel, if capital-intensive, approach. It only works if the market in Bordeaux stays strong, but when it works, it is dazzling. He buys more than he needs of the best Bordeaux he can afford. Later, when the wine has appreciated in value, he sells or trades his excess cases. The profits from these transactions often pay for the bottles he keeps from the original purchase.

He bought three cases of Château Latour 1990 for $800 a case when it was first available and ended up selling one case back to the retailer for $3,400. He paid for his remaining two cases of Château Latour and earned a profit of $1,000.

Other wines at other times would not appreciate nearly so dramatically. This collector is also lucky to be able to leave the tricky legalities to a professional, having found a retailer willing to deal with his wines on a consignment basis. Private parties cannot sell wine in most states.

The Essence

Learn how to taste, if for no other reason than to be able to hold your own against wine snobs when you encounter them. Swirl the wine around in the glass to make it evaporate faster and concentrate its aroma. When tasting critically, slurp the wine to aerate it, which intensifies your flavor perception. We all have varying levels of sensitivity to each tiny flavor component in wine, and therefore we each have at least a slightly different reaction to every wine.

The first question to ask is "Do I like it?" The next is "How much do I like it?" And finally, the big question is "What is it about this wine that I like or dislike?"

To address the last question sensibly, concentrate first on the weight and texture of the wine, then take note of the aromas and flavors you perceive, and finally (appropriately enough) consider the finish. A good wine leaves lots of flavor that seems to echo in the mouth.

CHAPTER NINE

How to Taste

Do you listen to music with an ear for how beautifully each player contributes to the whole, and for the structure of the composition and the niceties of the harmonic changes? Or do you let it wash over you and make you smile? When you watch baseball, do you keep score? Follow the changing situation as the batter works deeper into the count? Note how much the infield shifts when the batter turns to bunt? Or do you just enjoy the atmosphere and wait to cheer when the home team scores? With wine, the same options apply. You can slosh it down without a second thought except for how good it tastes with dinner, or you can pay attention to the details. There is no right way, only what you find most satisfying.

Even if you don't taste critically at the dinner table, there are several good reasons to learn how to do it. For one thing, you will never be tongue-tied at wine tastings and dinners, even those with wine snobs present. You will see pretension for what it is and never be intimidated by it. Learning a little about tasting lets you communicate your preferences to wine shop clerks and sommeliers. Best of all, you will learn what you like best and why, so you can duplicate and increase your pleasure.

Another good thing about wine tasting: You get to drink a lot of different wines.

Your tasting apparatus

We are all equipped with more or less the same number of taste buds. In recent years, scientists have discovered that some people have more taste buds than others. These people are called supertasters. Food seems much more intense to them. But taste buds only give us a small piece of the overall picture. Your tongue and mouth can only taste sweet, sour, salty and bitter, plus a lesser-understood fifth taste called *umami* (see chapters 6 and 11). Another sense organ captures all those little nuances that make up what we think of as flavor—what makes a potato taste like a potato instead of a carrot, and a Cabernet like a Cabernet instead of a Grenache. It's an area located at the back of the nose, which is one reason tasters pay so much attention to sniffing a glass of wine.

This dime-sized patch lies midway between the back of the nose and the back of the upper palate, an ideal spot for the air we breathe to waft past when we inhale. (However, if the nose is blocked, as when we have a cold, the air can't get to this sensory patch, and all those nuances are wasted. That's the logic behind the school science experiment in which you can't tell the difference between an onion and an apple when you close your eyes and hold your nose.)

To the untrained eye, wine tasters go through some strange gymnastics to give this sensory apparatus a full chance to pick up every trace of taste and aroma in a wine. But it makes sense when you think about the physiology behind it. Here is the standard winetasting procedure, step by step:

1. Swirling and sniffing

Swirling the wine around in the glass makes more of it evaporate as it splashes against the inside of the glass. As the

wine evaporates, the air carries hundreds of different molecules that make up the aroma, making it easier for you to sense them by sniffing at the wine. Smelling the wine before tasting it isolates these aromatics so you can perceive them without having to worry about alcohol, acidity or tannin.

Swirling the wine in the glass becomes second nature

SWIRLING.

to those of us who taste wine regularly, so much so that we do it unthinkingly with other beverages. It's a Pavlovian response: See a stemmed glass, swirl the contents. I've caught myself swirling orange juice, iced tea and water. My favorite

SNIFFING.

moment was when my friend Dan, at his Jewish wedding, took the glass of sacramental wine from the rabbi and proceed to swirl and sniff it. He has a picture of the rabbi peering at him incredulously over his prayer book. What was Dan going to do, send it back? His friends and family have kidded him mercilessly ever since.

2. Slurping

Take a sip and, holding the wine on the tongue, purse the lips as if to whistle, but instead of breathing out, breathe in. This agitates the wine in the mouth, literally aerating it. As it bubbles, it makes a distinctive gurgling sound. This is what

tickles the uninitiated more than anything else that wine tasters do, but now that we know about the tasting apparatus, it makes perfect sense. By agitating the wine and accelerating the evaporation process, we give that dime-sized sensory patch the full impact of all the aromatic molecules,

SLURPING.

while at the same time the tongue is appraising the acidity, sweetness, alcohol, bitterness and texture of the wine.

It takes a certain amount of confidence (or stupidity) to do this at the dinner table. If you're among friends who also taste wine regularly, no one will mind. Aunt Mabel will never understand.

Sensitivities

Tasting is an intensely personal experience. We might eat food and drink wine in the company of others, but no one else perceives them exactly the way you do. I cannot emphasize this enough. We might both be enjoying a Chardonnay equally. I might comment on its steely acidity. You might say it tastes a little sweet to you. I might note its pleasant peach-like flavor. You might say, no, it tastes more like pears and hazelnuts. Are we nuts? No we're human. Each of us tastes things with different perceptions.

The key here is thresholds. We are each sensitive to every element present in wine to a different degree. I hate to eat kidneys because to me they smell like the lion cage at the zoo. Others relish the taste, and don't get the leonine character I perceive so forcibly. A similar sort of gamy aroma can be present in some wines, particularly older Rhône reds. Some people hate it because it overwhelms the other flavors in the wine. Others, not as sensitive to it, like what it adds to the mix.

Because so many different flavors are swirling around in wine, our individual sensitivity to each of them affects our perceptions of all the others. So don't worry if you taste something others don't. Consider it something extra to talk about.

There is a product imported from France, called *Le Nez du Vin*, a collection of little vials containing esters of characteristic wine aromas. It's a good, if highly esoteric, way to get the characteristics fixed in your mind.

Temperature

Cold enhances bitterness in wine; warmth emphasizes sweetness and makes alcohol more prominent. At 72°F., normal American room temperature, a red wine may seem thin and hot, but at 65°F it becomes supple and fluid, and at 50°F decidedly tough and astringent. Thus, to minimize the astringency of a powerful, tannic red, pour the wine warm enough, but not so warm as to emphasize its alcohol. Drink sweet white wines well chilled to keep their sweetness in balance.

In general, serve full-bodied and mature red wines at 60°F to 65°F, light-bodied young reds at 55°F to 60°F, dry whites at 45°F to 50°F, and sweet whites at 40°F to 50°F. In a typical dining room heated to 70°F or higher, wine warms up in the glass fairly quickly. It's better to serve it a couple of degrees too cold than too warm.

Glasses

For tasting purposes, a standard all-purpose glass of 7 to 10 ounces does fine. Anything smaller tends to sap the goodness from more flavorful wines.

There is a smaller glass, called the INAO glass after the French organization that designed it some years ago. It's convenient because it's small enough to fit more glasses on the table, but after one becomes accustomed to drinking wine out of larger glasses, it seems puny.

Various glassmakers have come up with tasting glasses, often in unusual shapes. I especially like one called *Le Taster* by the French company Impitoyable. Made of fine crystal, it looks like a short tumbler with a big dimple in the middle of the base, another dimple in the side, and a rim that narrows like a standard tulip glass. The glass is held with thumb and finger in the dimples. To me, it has the effect of delivering the aromas and flavors in the wine with digital clarity, like a compact disc as compared

to a normal wine glass's cassette tape. (It delivers the flaws along with the better elements in a wine, which is why it's called *"impitoyable"* — French for pitiless.)

Of course you would not use a glass like this at table. But for professional tasting, it's unbeatable.

Order of tasting

In an organized tasting of several wines, one wine affects the taste of the wines that follow it. This works on different elements. For example, the residue of tannin from a very tannic wine can make the next wine seem more tannic than it really is. Following a wine with high acidity, a normally balanced wine can seem insipid. A low-acid wine can make the next one seem overly sharp. Sweetness in one wine can make the next one seem sour.

Several tactics can help you avoid these pitfalls. The easiest is to take the time to let your senses recover between one wine and the next. A bite or two of bread and a sip of water can clear the palate. I like sparkling water, especially neutral-tasting seltzer, which seems to scrub away the tannins from red wine as they collect in my mouth. (Champagne can do the same at the dinner table.)

If a bite of bread or a sip of sparkling water fails to refresh a tannin-coated palate, it's time to take matters into your own hands. In long tastings with lots of young red wines, I have been known to use a clean, dry paper towel or cloth napkin to blot my tongue, inner cheeks and upper palate. I would not, I hasten to add, do this at the dinner table, but in a professional tasting, you do whatever works.

Atmosphere

In a professional tasting, silence rules. Conversation is distracting. Concentration is everything. You want the surroundings to be as neutral as possible, ideally with white surfaces, odor-free air, cool room temperature. It is not fun.

In a wine tasting with friends, such obsession would be out of place. You can be as serious or as casual as you like.

White tablecloths and napkins are nice, the better to see the wines' actual color. Conversation is fine, but if you're trying to rate wines for your own future reference, it would be prudent if no one tried to influence you until you arrive at your own opinion. After that, it's OK to focus the conversation on the wine, since it's what everyone is there for. At dinner, most people would consider it obnoxious to talk only about the wine.

Swallowing vs. spitting

In a tasting of more than a few wines, you must decide whether to drink the wines or spit them out as you taste them. Newcomers to wine always feel weird about that. Didn't your mother teach you never to spit anything out in front of other people? Trust me, it's OK in a wine tasting. This is why.

Let's say you're tasting eight wines and you have two ounces in each glass, a modest pour. You taste all the wines, go back and compare No. 5 to No. 2, and on and on until you finish all the wine. You have consumed, without benefit of food, about two-thirds of a bottle. With so much alcohol in your system, your sensitivity and judgment started becoming impaired along about wine No. 4.

Some people address this problem by taking little tiny baby sips to minimize the alcohol absorption. I don't know

about you, but I can't get the true taste of the wine unless I have at least a couple of teaspoons of it in my mouth. To get a handle on any wine, I need to sip it two or three times, and if I want to compare it to any other wines side by side, the number of sips has ballooned to five, six, or seven. The only way to do that and keep my head as clear for wine No. 8 as it was for wine No. 1 is to spit.

Spitting can be done discreetly using an opaque tumbler (so you don't see the expectorated wine). As it fills up, it can then be emptied into a larger bucket. Or you can station a large bucket on a stand next to your chair. Either way, serious wine tasters will not object. Again, do not attempt this at the dinner table.

What to taste for

I have read books that purport to teach wine tasting, and watched educators initiate unsuspecting students in the rites and rituals of wine tasting, and for my money they all get it backwards. They all try to get you to put off making up your mind about how much you like the wine until after you have assessed every last detail of the wine.

Baloney. You wouldn't be human if you didn't form an initial impression of a wine as soon as you took that first sip. That impression could change in the next few minutes, as you let the wine's characteristics play out, or as you take another sip. But the most important question about any wine is: How much do I like it? Only after you've reached at least a tentative opinion should you ask the next question: What is it about this wine that I like or dislike?

And that's why we do all that gazing at the color, sniffing at the aromas and swirling of wine around in the mouth—to figure out what the wine has that makes us like it or not. Tasting means making a series of assessments. For my money, the ones that count the most are (a) the weight and texture of the wine, (b) the nature and intensity of aromas and flavors, and finally (c) the finish and aftertaste.

Weight and texture

This is another way to describe what wine tasters mean when they talk about structure. It's the bones of the wine, the way it's built. Some wines feel heavy, others feel light. The main factor is the alcohol content, but deft winemaking can hide the alcohol, the way some big men can dance as if they are light on their feet. Some wines feel rough, others smooth. The prime reason here is tannin. Some tannins feel rougher than others, and savvy winemaking can manage the tannins to make them feel plush as a velvet sofa instead of scratchy like a wire brush.

The weight and texture of a wine reflect the way the acidity and alcohol balance with the tannin, among other factors, one of which is...

Intensity of aromas and flavors

Sometimes you stick your nose in the glass and all you smell is—nothing. Sometimes a hundred aromas seem to jump out of the glass. It's the difference between a sunny sky with a few fleecy clouds and a riotous sunset reflecting gold, crimson and purple hues off of fascinating-shaped clouds. That's intensity.

Every wine has a flavor profile. When I try to paint a descriptive profile of a wine, I am particularly interested in noting the flavors that make it distinctive. Some Chardonnays taste like pineapple. Others taste like peaches. Still others are more reminiscent of green apples or citrus. Some have spice or vanilla nuances from aging in oak barrels. Others pick up earthy or nutty flavors from specific fermentation techniques. Every wine type has its own flavor range, some wider than others. Tasting is the best way to get to know them.

Flavors that appear in wine

The grape is an amazing fruit. Off the vine it can have flavors that are reminiscent of other fruits. I have picked Shiraz grapes in Australia that taste like plums. Muscat

grapes taste remarkably like litchi fruit. Sauvignon Blanc grapes can be distinctly reminiscent of newly mown grass or freshly cut herbs.

In wine the possibilities multiply, as the chemistry of fermentation creates new molecules in the finished wine. These molecules are often identical to those that give the characteristic flavors to these other fruits and vegetables. So if you taste strawberry in that glass of Pinot, it's not just an overactive imagination.

Finish and aftertaste

After swallowing or spitting, a good wine leaves a lasting impression. Mediocre wines just fade away and bad wines make you want to wash out your mouth. But the flavors of a good wine keep echoing in the mouth pleasantly. This is called the finish, and I strongly recommend paying close attention to it. If you find lots of good flavor and it lasts a long time, that's a great finish.

Even if a first sip strikes you as awkward or odd, often a wine seems to come together on the finish. This is a sign that it will only get better with a little more age. Even a few more minutes in the glass can let all the flavors permeate the wine.

Notes and ratings: Remembering the moment

I know some very good tasters who never take notes. But they are few and far between. If you want to keep 'em straight in your mind, you'll probably want to take notes, at least at formal tastings. Write down whatever you find most distinc-

CHECKLIST OF AROMAS

Fruity
Berry
  Blackberry
  Boysenberry
  Fresh Currant
  Raspberry
  Strawberry
Stone Fruit
  Apricot
  Cherry
  Litchi
  Olive
  Peach
  Plum
Tropical Fruit
  Guava
  Papaya
  Passion fruit
  Pineapple
Other Fruit
  Apple (green, golden, baked)
  Fig
  Grapefruit
  Lemon
  Lime
  Melon
  Pear
  Quince

Vegetal/Herbal
Vegetable
  Asparagus
  Green bean
  Mushroom
  Rhubarb
  Sweet Anise
  Sweet pepper
Herb
  Dill
  Eucalyptus
  Mint
  Pine needle
  Sage
  Tea leaf
  Tobacco

Floral
  Orange blossom
  Rose petal
  Violet

Nut/Spice
Nut
  Almond
  Hazelnut
  Walnut
Spice
  Clove
  Licorice
  Nutmeg
  Pepper
  Vanilla

Sweet
  Butter
  Butterscotch
  Caramel
  Chocolate
  Cream
  Honey
  Molasses

Earthy/Woody
  Burnt wood
  Coffee
  Forest floor
  Game
  Smoke
  Wet wood

Chemical
Petroleum
  Kerosene
  Plastic
  Tar
Sulfur
  Burnt match
    (sulfur dioxide)
  Rotten egg
Animal
  Horse
  Leather
  Sauerkraut
  Wet wool
  Yeast (like baked bread)

tive about the wine, the characteristics that will best remind you of it when you read your notes several months or several years later. Most tasters do this in a systematic manner, first noting the color, then first impressions of the aroma, followed by a general description of the structure, flavor, finish, and perhaps a general comment or two.

Color can range from pale straw to deep gold in a white wine, from light garnet to deep ruby in a red. Personally, I don't care much about color, except to note if it is particularly light or dark. But if you want to get a good look at the color, don't hold the glass up to the light. Tilt it away from you at about a 45° angle and look at it against a white tablecloth or a piece of white paper.

Aroma is more important, particularly if something stands out, such as the smell of oak, game or herbs. But all that comes with the taste anyway.

Structure is the framework of a wine, the skeleton and musculature that support the skin of the flavors. A combination of alcohol, acidity, sweetness and tannin in the wine, the structure should not stand out. In a good wine, the structure reveals itself in texture and balance. If a wine feels out of balance, make a note of what's sticking out — is it too sharp? too flabby? too rough? too hot? If it's in balance, is the overall impression lean and sleek or rich and plush? See the glossary for more tasting terms.

Flavor is the other big factor. Every wine has a flavor profile. Note whatever seems distinctive about it to you, and what sort of flavors persist after you sip. That's the finish, and really good wines deliver whole paragraphs on the finish.

To rate or not to rate

Everyone rates wine, even those who vehemently protest that they don't. "I like it" and "I don't like it" is basically a two-point rating system. As soon as you say "I like this one better than that one," you're rating the wines. Distilling those preferences into a rating, whether it's four stars, five grape bunches, or 10, 20 or 100 points, is only a matter of how fine you want to make the gradations.

Use whatever system you feel most comfortable with. At informal tastings where I don't have time or the state of mind to be very precise, I just use a series of plus or minus signs. One plus sign means I like it, two means I like it a lot, and three means "wow!" The minus signs go the other direction. But do use something so that, when you look over your notes a week, a month or a year later, you can remember just which wines you liked, and how much.

About ratings

At *Wine Spectator*, we are frequently asked about how exactly we arrive at our scores, and what those scores mean. First, we only rate new wines if we can taste them blind. This means that the taster or tasters never know the name of the wine or the price when they award the scores. We do frequently go back and modify the tasting *note* after finding out the name of the wine. This is so that the note can put the wine in context, commenting on its relative value or how it might compare to past vintages of the same wine.

Tastings are done by up to three tasters, all full-time editors for the magazine. When several tasters are involved, one is designated the chief taster and takes into account the others' comments and scores before recording the appropriate score. We do not use a formal system of awarding so many points for aroma, body, flavor, finish and so on, but we consider all of these factors and more before settling on a score. You could compare it to grading an essay test. It's not a mathematical process, but a subjective one done by experienced people.

To answer another frequently asked question, a lower score for a famous, expensive wine than for a newly released, unheralded wine does in fact mean that we think the higher-scored wine is a better, more pleasurable wine. Because the wine is tasted blind, however, the score cannot account for the intellectual and emotional satisfaction that a wine such a 1945 Bordeaux might deliver.

Why the 100-point scale makes sense

Wine Spectator uses a 100-point scale because it's intuitive. Anyone who attended school in the United States knows that 100 points on a test or essay is perfect, 90 is an A, 80 is a B, and 70 is a C. If you don't like numbers, use the letter grades. If you think ten points of gradation between an A grade and a B grade makes too fine a distinction, just use 80, 85 and 90.

One of the most common questions we get about the rating scale is, "How much difference is there between a wine that rates 89 and one that rates 88?" The answer is, very little. And that's why I prefer the 100-point scale for rating the thousands of wines that we taste every year at the magazine. Any other system is too crude for dealing with so many wines. Here's why:

Take the 549 California Chardonnays *Wine Spectator* reviewed in 1998. Let's say you ranked them all in order of preference. You would have a sort of continuum, a lineup in which your opinion of the individual wines' quality diminished as you went down the line. You could sort them into groups, giving the best group five stars, the next group four stars, and so on. But you would have some tough choices, because the best four-star wines would be almost as good as the ones that barely made it into the five-star category.

The 100-point scale encompasses the best of both worlds.

By relating the rating to letter grades in school, you can tell that wines scoring in the 90s are the A wines, and ones that score in 80s are the Bs. But you can also tell that the taster liked the ones that score 90 or 91 just a little better than the ones that score 88 or 89, important information if you're relating quality to price (see Q/PR, page 180).

In Europe, professionals often judge wines on a 30-point scale, which happens to be the same range used in their schools. Wine professionals often learn a 20-point scale in enology and viticulture school, which many writers and wine fanciers also like to use. A 10-point scale works better for some.

Traditionally, most tasters allot 20 percent of their score to color, 30 percent to aroma and 50 percent to flavor. Some vary it by allotting 40 percent to flavor and 10 percent to "overall quality," which reveals the true purpose of rating scales: to reflect how much you really like the wine. So take my advice: pay attention to color, carefully analyze the aroma and judiciously assess the flavor, but in the end, make sure any rating reflects your overall preference.

Tasting opportunities

Even if you don't buy a bunch of wines and set up your own tasting, take every chance you get to sample a variety of wines, the better to build up your tasting experience. Winery tasting rooms offer an obvious venue. Although laws vary from state to state, many wine shops have a few bottles open for customers to try, often without charge. Restaurants often have interesting wines by the glass. Avail yourself of the chance to try something different.

Organized tastings by wineries, wine shops, restaurants and private wine clubs can provide more opportunities to add to your background. Big walk-around tastings often have plenty of different wines available. Although a noisy, crowded party atmosphere is not the best for critical tasting, you can get a general impression of a lot of different wines in one fell swoop and have fun in the process.

How to set up your own tasting

An easy approach is to ask each person to bring a wine that fits a theme of your selection. Maybe it would be as general as world Sauvignon Blancs or as specific as Sancerre, which is made from Sauvignon Blanc in a specific region of France. I would choose something that you are not terribly familiar with, so there will be a greater sense of discovery.

As for food, have just bread and crackers at first, but after everyone has had a chance to taste the wines bring out something more substantial. To keep it simple, you could just have cold food, or if you prefer cook something that might taste good with the wines. Just remember, taste first, then enjoy the wines with food.

Ideally each person should have a glass for each wine, up to six to eight glasses. If you're tasting more wines, then divide the wines and taste by "flight," which means a group of wines representing a portion of the total. You can use just one glass per person, but this makes it a little harder to compare wines, and if you keep re-pouring so that the tasters can compare a later wine with an earlier one, you'll run out of wine more quickly. Many wine-tasting groups have each

member bring his/her own glasses so you won't have to stockpile stemware. You can get a carrier that holds six to eight glasses.

At tastings, I prefer to rinse with wine rather than water. Even "clean" glasses can retain unwinelike smells from the water used to wash them. On visits to Italy I learned how to put a tiny splash of the first wine to be poured in the first glass, swirl it around, and pour it into the next glass, continuing until all the glasses have been rinsed with the wine. It's better than diluting the next wine with water from a rinse. When it is necessary to use the same glass for the next wine, just empty your glass well and refill it with the next pour.

In vertical tastings (a series of different vintages of the same wine), conventional wisdom moves from youngest to oldest in chronological order, under the assumption that the wines will increase in complexity and interest with age. Some contrarians prefer to move from oldest to youngest, on the theory that the younger, more tannic wines would blunt the palate for the more subtle older wines if tasted before them. Finally, in large tastings, it's a good idea to group the vintages by style—the lighter, perhaps lesser, ones together, the more structured and more famous ones afterward.

There are merits to all three approaches. Starting with the youngest works best if none of the wines is older than 10 or 15 years. Starting with oldest works best if there are some old, delicate wines in the group. Grouping by style requires a certain amount of knowledge, but if someone has done his homework, that's the approach I prefer.

The Bipin approach

Bipin Desai, a serious collector who stages long and elaborate tastings, has perfected my favorite approach involving a meal. He approaches a restaurant with the idea of creating a menu to serve with the wines, which he organizes into smaller flights. In an extensive vertical tasting, each flight represents a mini-vertical within the larger context. For example, in a vertical tasting of Château Latour, Desai will save the greatest vintages to taste side by side in the final flight. The weaker vintages go into a catch-all flight at the beginning. The rest can be organized into decades, and then it's up to the chef to create a different dish for each flight.

Before each course, the wines come out first so everyone can taste them without the distraction of food. (When this is done for large groups, volunteer sommeliers at a side table pour the wines into glasses already tagged with the vintage. Then they bring out a whole set for each person.) When the food arrives, everyone can enjoy the wines for what they were intended to do, which is to consume with dinner.

Planning your own wine tasting dinner

First, keep the food simple. That takes pressure off you, or whomever is cooking, and lets the wines shine without competition. Keep the wines related—say, several versions of the same varietal, or different vintages from the same producer. That makes it easier to compare and contrast.

Serve only six to eight wines. For most people, serve three sets of two wines, or two sets of three, depending on your menu. That way you can concentrate on all the wines without getting overwhelmed.

Finally, make sure everybody talks. Remember, there are no right answers. What each person likes best is right for him or her. Stimulating conversation and learning are legitimate goals of a wine tasting dinner. Most of all, have fun.

The Essence

I find it useful to divide the universe of wine into everyday wines, weekend wines (which deliver more complexity and refinement) and special occasion wines (which provide a memorable experience). Connoisseurs keep an open mind and can appreciate how well a wine in each category performs. Snobs only drink what they think they should.

Better wines generally cost more, but you can find a wide range of quality within every price range. These ranges overlap. Smart wine buyers pick from the high end of the quality range at any given price. In theory, and often in reality, a $10 wine can be better than a $60 wine. A wine's price often depends on rarity and regional reputation rather than purely on quality. Less expensive wines from lesser-known regions often are better than expensive wines with better-known labels. They can also be more drinkable earlier than expensive wines built to age.

By actually comparing wines of differing prices, you can discover the wines you really like, and seek them out.

CHAPTER TEN

How Good Is It?

Wherever a wine comes from and however it was made, ultimately you must pay for the privilege of drinking it. Those of us who review wine for a living do it to sort out the ones that are worth it. This annoys a certain segment of the wine-drinking public, who argue that rating wines makes about as much sense as rating works of art. If you don't rate Picassos, why rate wines?

The answer, for me, is that no one asks you to pony up tens, even hundreds, of dollars to get a look at a Picasso. You go to a museum, pay a nominal fee to get in, walk up to the painting, and drink it in for as long as you like. If we must pay for the privilege of consuming wine, we have every right to determine if it's worth the price. In the end, it's your decision, so it's worth thinking about how to do it.

I find it useful to divide the universe of wine into three levels.

• **Everyday wines:** Most wines fall into this category—sound wines with appealing flavors, the vinous equivalent of background music. Everyday wine should not stretch your budget, just provide enough quality to make an amiable companion to dinner.

• **Weekend wines:** These deliver more complex flavors and a little more refinement than your basic everyday wine. They have a bit more of a sense of celebration about them. Maybe they have been in the cellar for a year or two getting a little better with age.

• **Special occasion wines:** These are jewels, the ones that lift wine from a beverage to a memorable experience. You save these for anniversaries, birthdays, great dinners.

Being a connoisseur without being snobbish

Snobs won't drink anything less than what they consider "the best," or perhaps the trendiest wines of the moment.

Snobs don't realize that quality can be found in the vinous equivalent of jeans and a casual shirt when the occasion calls for it. In short, snobs don't understand that the glory of wine is in its diversity, the many personalities it can show. Some snobs only drink expensive wine, limiting their choices to the relatively few that have some sort of interna-

---

RECOMMENDED WINES

In the real world, you can impress a client, your boss or your wine-savvy date by fitting the wine choice to the occasion. Here's a short list of recommended wines for the three levels of wine. This is by no means an exhaustive list, offering only one wine for each type and each category.

EVERYDAY WINES

Red

Bordeaux: Château d'Arche (Haut-Médoc)
Rhône: Jaboulet Aîné Parallèle 45
Piedmontese red: Michele Chiarlo Barbera d'Asti
Tuscan red: Cecchi Chianti Classico
Spanish red: Bodegas Palacios Remondo Rioja Crianza
Cabernet Sauvignon: Hess Select (California)
Merlot: Concha y Toro Trio (Chile)
Pinot Noir: Anapamu Monterey County (California)
Other red: Rosemount Shiraz Diamond Label (Australia)

White

Alsace: Pierre Sparr Pinot Gris
Italian white: Bollini Pinot Grigio
Chardonnay: Lindemans Bin 65 (Australia)
Riesling: Columbia (Washington)
Sparkling: Korbel Natural (California)

WEEKEND WINES

Red

Bordeaux: Château Haut-Bages Libéral (Pauillac)
Red Burgundy: Marquis d'Angerville Volnay Premier Cru
Rhône: Alain Graillot Crozes-Hermitage
Piedmontese red: Beni di Batasiolo Barbaresco
Tuscan red: Fontodi Chianti Classico Riserva

tional stamp of approval, believing that inexpensive wines can't be good. I also know snobs in reverse who only drink inexpensive wines, believing that expensive wines can't possibly be worth the cost.

Ultimately, the difference between a connoisseur and a snob is that the connoisseur keeps an open mind and recog-

---

Cabernet Sauvignon: Beringer Knights Valley (California)
Merlot: Columbia Crest Reserve (Washington)
Pinot Noir: Sanford Santa Barbara County (California)
Other red: Ridge Lytton Springs (California Zinfandel)

White
White Burgundy: Verget Bourgogne White
Alsace: Domaine Ostertag Riesling
Italian white: Terruzzi & Puthod Terre di Tufo
Chardonnay: Ferrari-Carano Alexander Valley (California)
Riesling: Grosset Clare Valley Polish Hill (Australia)
Other white: Château Carbonnieux (Bordeaux white)
Sparkling: Roederer Estate L'Ermitage (California)

SPECIAL OCCASION WINES

Red
Bordeaux: Château Margaux
Red Burgundy: Jadot Beaune Premier Cru Clos des Ursules
Rhône: E. Guigal Côte-Rôtie Côtes Brune et Blonde
Piedmontese red: Prunotto Barolo Bussia
Tuscan red: Sassicaia
Cabernet Sauvignon: Dominus (California)
Merlot: Matanzas Creek (California)
Pinot Noir: Beaux Frères (Oregon)
Other red: Vega Sicilia Unico (Spain)

White
White Burgundy: Chartron & Trebuchet Puligny-Montrachet
Alsace: Hugel Gewürztraminer Alsace Jubilée
Italian white: Ornellaia Sauvignon Toscana Poggio alle Gazze
Chardonnay: Robert Mondavi Reserve (California)
Riesling: J.J. Prüm Riesling Spätlese Graacher Himmelreich (Mosel)
Other white: Didier Dagueneau Pouilly-Fumé Pur Sang (France)
Sparkling: Veuve Clicquot Champagne Brut La Grand
    Dame (France)

THE FAMOUS BORDEAUX CLASSIFICATION OF 1855—AS FANCIFULLY DEPICTED HERE BY THE ARTIST CARL LAUBIN IN *LES GRAND CRUS CLASSÉS DU MEDOC EN 1855*—WAS AN EARLY ATTEMPT TO RATE VARIOUS WINERIES' PRODUCT. IRONICALLY, THE RANKING WAS ACTUALLY BASED ON THE MARKET VALUE OF EACH ESTATE'S OUTPUT.

nizes quality no matter where it comes from or who made it. Snobs only drink what they think they should.

A true connoisseur understands and appreciates wine without becoming obnoxious about it. Part of it is knowing when to stop talking about wine before you bore others. But for me, the key is to respect each individual's taste. Offer the best wines you can to your guests, choose the best wines for the price on a wine list, but remember that someone who prefers wine to be a little sweet probably won't enjoy that tart little Riesling Trocken that sounds just perfect to you.

Yes, there is such a thing as absolute quality

Like playing in tune and keeping the beat in music, a good wine needs to fulfill certain requirements. It must be free of faults, or at least hide successfully whatever minor faults it might have. Beyond the basics, though, there are some important elements that define quality. One is crafts-manship—the winemaker's technical ability to capture appealing and distinctive aromas and flavors in a frame-work that feels balanced, and to allow those flavors to echo deliciously in the mouth for more than a few seconds after you swallow it. In a really good wine, those aromas and fla-vors come together in a way that expresses something more than the flavors of the grape. The more nuances you can detect, the more complex the wine.

Whether you like those flavors is another matter. But if a wine shows a range of aromas and flavors and it doesn't taste like every other wine, and if those flavors persist in the mouth after you swallow the wine, that's a measure of absolute quality.

And sometimes you just throw out the rules

Remember Joe Cocker? He was a singer in the 1960s who did everything wrong. He sounded hoarse. He croaked on high notes. He slurred words. But he had a huge hit in "You Are So Beautiful" because there was something in his performance that absolutely defined soul. The wine equiv-alent of that is a funky old Châteauneuf-du-Pape that reeks of mushroom, farmyard and game smells, tastes like some-one filtered it through potting soil, and maybe folds in a touch of vinegariness on the finish. And yet, its soul emerges with such force, it's unmistakable.

Singers like Cocker and wines like that Châteauneuf-du-Pape are exceptions, however. Compensating factors are rarely found for what some perceive as technical faults, but it happens. And just as musical purists hated Joe Cocker, wine purists hate those funky wines. That's OK. More for the rest of us.

What goes into wine quality

To get special character into a wine demands extra attention all along the winemaking process. The best wines result from the winemaker carefully managing every aspect—knowing when to intervene and when to let the wine alone, and how to tweak the wine to get the most out of it. It costs more to keep grape yields down in the vineyard (to intensify flavor in the remaining grapes), to wait for riper grapes (and risk losing the harvest to bad weather), to use a large percentage of new barrels every year, to select only the barrels and vats that have the best wine, to hold a wine a little longer so it's readier upon release, to ship it in refrigerated containers so it won't spoil in summer's heat. These are just a few of the things that can affect that moment the wine touches your lips.

Modern winemaking allows for cost-saving compromises that can lower quality. Clever trellising systems can extract more juice from a vineyard. Tossing a bag of oak chips into a fermentation vat can approximate the flavor that comes from barrel aging, but it can't reproduce the texture. Shortening fermentation can make a wine ready to drink sooner. Blending in lesser wines can stretch the good stuff past the point where it delivers all the pleasure it can. These things can affect the moment the wine touches your lips, too.

For more details, see chapter 4, "Why Wine Tastes Like It Does."

Q/PR (Quality/Price Ratio)— an individual preference

What makes one wine worth $60 a bottle when another, made from the same grape from the same region, carries a

$10 price tag? That's one of the maddening questions about wine, because there is no guarantee that the $60 wine will please you more. In fact, whenever we plunk down our money (on anything, not just wine), we all calculate whether it was worth the price. With thousands of wines to choose from, varying so much in price and quality, this Quality-to-Price Ratio (Q/PR) is critical. The better the quality, the lower the price, the higher the ratio.

Ultimately, this gets down to a very personal question of taste. Expensive wines justify their cost by being more complex, more distinctive. By definition, the wider the range of flavors in a product, the more an individual is likely to find something not to like. That's why fast food tastes so blah — it's made to offend the fewest people. Just as you might prefer folk songs to opera, you might well find you like the $10 wine better than the $60 bottle. This is good news. You just saved $50.

My theory of overlapping price and quality ranges

In the scheme of things, better wines generally cost more. But at every price level, there are overachievers and underachievers. And just as you will find a range of quality at every price, so there is a range of prices at every quality level. These ranges overlap. The best of the less-expensive wines are better than the worst of the more-expensive wines. That's the key. Smart wine buyers pick from the high end of the quality range at any given price.

Here, for example, are three actual 1994 wines from a recent *Wine Spectator* report on California Cabernet Sauvignon. Each cost $45 to $50 at the time of its release in 1998. (The reviews are by James Laube, *Wine Spectator's* senior editor who specializes in California wine.)

Bell Baritelle Vineyard *$50*   Medium-weight, with supple cedar, sage and currant flavors and finishing with a hint of spice, but overall it lacks intensity, focus and concentration. Drink now. **82** points (or "good").

Silver Oak *$45*   Combines ripe, rich, complex fruit with a sense of finesse and harmony. The core of anise, currant, sage and cedar unfolds to reveal more depth and complexity. Finishes with a long, satisfying aftertaste. Best now through 2006. **89** points (or "very good," almost "outstanding").

Arrowood Reserve Speciale *$50*   Beautifully crafted, complex and concentrated, with a tightly focused core of earthy currant, black cherry, cedary oak and spicy nuances, turning long and full on the finish. Best from 2001 through 2010. **94** points (or "outstanding," almost "classic").

I would happily drink any one of them if you handed me a glass. Which one would you buy? On a simple rating vs. price comparison, Arrowood wins. But wait. If you don't want to wait several years to drink it, the Silver Oak delivers more of what you want for your money right now. The Bell Baritelle Vineyard, on the other hand, does not read like a $50 wine. At that price, you can find much better wines from 1994, which was a great vintage for California Cabernet.

How can a $10 wine be better than a $60 wine?

It happens more than you think. Year in and year out, for example, I rate Rosemount Shiraz Diamond Label from Australia 90 points, give or take a point or two. You can often find it priced in discount stores at less than $10. At the same time, plenty of underachieving Bordeaux, Burgundies and California Cabernets (even some other Australian Shirazes) carry price tags of $60 or more. Yet on an absolute scale, the Rosemount is better. It has richer flavor, more focused character, more depth, a longer finish — in short, all those things that determine quality.

So how do Bordeaux, Burgundy and California Cabernet producers justify this disparity? Well, the land is more costly and they use expensive barrels and bottles, but mostly it's reputation. Consumers of those wines seem willing to pay the price for them because these have proven to be the most desirable categories in most years. The best wines from the best vintages certainly deserve that reputation. They're Special Occasion Wines. In good vintages, the underachievers ride the coattails of the deserving wines, getting inflated prices because the whole category has cachet. In bad vintages, even the best wines don't deliver good Q/PR. There have been Bordeaux vintages in which none of the wines rated "outstanding," yet their prices were still in the $30 to $100 range—a case of Everyday Wines in Special Occasion Wines' clothing.

Consumers willing to take a chance on less-familiar regions, which have not achieved the cachet they deserve, can find great Q/PR. To do that, just open your mind to the possibilities.

How much is too much?

When two wines cost about the same but one gets a much higher rating, the choice is pretty simple. Personal taste determines where you draw the line when the more expensive wine is also better. If you're after the best (which should be whatever your palate tells you is the best), you often must dig a little deeper into your wallet to get it. But how much more?

Let's add another wine to that Cabernet comparison.

Groth Reserve *$100* Enormously complex, firm and tightly wound, with ripe, firm tannins and a wide range of rich, concentrated flavors, cherry, wild berry, plum, cedar, coffee and spice. Shows remarkable finesse and polish for a young wine. Tempting now for its suppleness, but sure to age for another decade; best from 2001 through 2009. **96** points (or "classic").

Groth gets 96 points and costs $50 more than Arrowood, which you might recall rated 94. Is two points worth 50 bucks? For some people, the answer is always no. But if the Groth style speaks your language, if you get a bigger thrill from drinking it than you do from the Arrowood, and you can afford the C-note for it, why not go for it? Unless you're

Bill Gates, they are both Special Occasion Wines.

The problem with $75 Cabernets and $50 Chardonnays is that it narrows the number of wine drinkers who can afford to drink them. At the risk of sounding like an old fogey, I remember writing an indignant column in 1980 wondering who could afford those appallingly high-priced new $10 Cabernets. No question, top-level wine has out-paced inflation by a wide margin.

When wine costs so much, production costs aren't the reason

Here's a little secret. It does not cost Groth twice as much to make its $100 Reserve as it costs Arrowood to make its $50 Reserve Spéciale. All the new barrels, fancy winemaking equipment and grapegrowing bills could be paid for if the wines sold for $25 or $30, and both produc-ers would still make a decent profit.

It's all about image. Wineries cite supply and demand, noting that it's a free market and if consumers are willing to pay the price, that's what the product is worth. All true. But you can also put the facts in a less flattering light. Wineries work hard to maintain their luxury image. It started with a few top California winemakers believing that their Cabernets were as good as Bordeaux, and pricing them to match. Angelo Gaja did the same thing in Italy. Pretty soon, anyone who wanted to be taken seriously as a first-rank winemaker raised prices to keep up.

You can't argue with success. The wines are good, and consumers have been willing to pay prices that, in a time of almost no inflation, shot up dramatically. Blame the wineries if you like, but we are the ones willing to fork over the cash.

The price of longevity and ageability

A wine need not be ageable to be good. Plenty of wines are gorgeous when you buy them and even though they might fade within a few years, they do deliver greatness. But longevity does influence a wine's price, though not neces-

WINE SPECTATOR RATES WINES AFTER TASTING THEM BLIND. YOU CAN TRY THIS AT HOME BY INVITING A FEW FRIENDS OVER AND ASKING EACH TO BRING A WINE "IN DISGUISE." IT'S A GREAT WAY TO TEST WHETHER YOUR PERCEPTION OF QUALITY IS INFLUENCED BY A WINE'S WELL-KNOWN NAME.

sarily its quality. From a practical standpoint, once you start amassing wine, whether in a closet or full-scale wine room, simple arithmetic dictates that you must drink some of it later rather than sooner. You want those wines to hold their qualities until you can get around to them. That's simple longevity. Ageability is when wines reward cellaring by developing a whole new range of delicious characteristics.

The great ones do this. Everyone knows which wines they are, and the price goes up accordingly.

If you prefer drinking wines young and have no intention of holding onto them for years and years before drinking them, think twice about paying that premium for longevity and ageability. Wines built for the long haul can also be a little rough to drink when they are young. Reds are packed with tannin. Whites carry high acidity. Some old-fashioned vintners still use a high level of sulfur dioxide at bottling to preserve wines longer. (It works, but it's not too pleasant when the wine is young.)

The antidote

Fortunately, there are still plenty of drinkable, rewarding wines available at relatively modest prices. You can prove it by setting up some comparative tastings for yourself. Choose two or three highly regarded wines of the same type, but at differing price levels. Have someone else pour them into identical glasses so you won't know which is which, and just taste them. That's the best way to discover what you really like. Do this on more than one occasion, because you will learn more about yourself every time.

You might discover that you like the accessibility of a less expensive wine. Or you might prefer the extra character of a more expensive product. Either way, you'll know what you like, not what someone else says you should like. And you'll be on your way to true connoisseurship.

The Essence

Remember that you will probably consume most wine without benefit of food. Sips taken before or after the dish is served and extra sips between bites easily outnumber those taken with food. For that reason, never choose a poor wine hoping the food will make it taste better. Drink a wine you like.

CRAB CAKES WITH BEURRE BLANC PAIRED WITH RIESLING.

Wine matches with food best when the size and weight of the wine balance with the richness and heartiness of the food. These elements are more important than any flavor associations, but if you do try to fine-tune the flavors focus on the key component in the food, which is not always the main ingredient. Most often, it's the sauce or seasoning.

In cooking with wine, use only wines good enough to drink, cook them long enough to evaporate most or all of the alcohol, and don't use too much wine, as the acidity in wine can throw a dish out of whack.

CHAPTER ELEVEN

Wine and Food Made Simple

Who decided that wine-and-food matching should be a chore? Read enough books and articles on the subject, sift through enough rules and helpful advice, and you might think it's better to forget the whole thing and drink a beer. So before this wine-and-food thing can form a black cloud over dinner, let's clear the air. As you read through this chapter, keep in mind one overriding criterion for matching food and wine. Engrave it on your wine cellar wall. Copies suitable for framing are available upon request.

Steiman's Central Premise

The object of the game is to enjoy the meal.
Therefore, drink the wine you like with the food you like.
All the rest is fine-tuning.

Those who wish to delve into it will find plenty of opportunity for fine-tuning. The possibilities for flawless matches are endless. But those who just want to wash down dinner with a compatible glass of wine can relax. Just follow the Central Premise. What's the worst that can happen? In the rare circumstance when the wine clashes with the food—and it is rare—you might need a swallow of water or a nibble of bread in between bites and sips. The point is, you will still enjoy dinner.

The First Principle

Always drink a better wine and sacrifice the food match rather than settle for a mediocre wine to make a good match.

One minor miracle of the dining table is that faulty wines can taste better with food. The textures and flavors of a meal can change the way we perceive the wine we drink with it. Experienced wine-and-food matchers know how to tweak the food to bring out the best in a wine. Or they can find just the right wine to be tweaked by the elements in the food.

This is advanced stuff, like learning how to place your lob in tennis. The important thing to remember is that it is, after all, fine tuning. Most of us are happy to place our tennis lobs so they fall in-bounds. Rest assured, any good wine will fall in-bounds. All it has to do is land on the table.

If the wine is good, a bad match will not destroy dinner. The reason is so obvious I wonder if most of those writing about food and wine even notice. To wit:

Most wine is consumed without food

Consider the usual scenario. You have carefully selected a 10-year-old Cabernet to drink with your lamb chops with red wine sauce because Cabernet matches up well with lamb. You pour the wine and take a few sips, admiring the way it has aged. You take a bite of food and a sip of wine. And another sip, because the wine is so good. And so on. How many bites in an average serving of lamb chops? Eight? Ten? How many sips of wine in the eight ounces of Cabernet in the two glasses you might consume with the lamb? Allowing two teaspoons per sip (a generous gulp, actually), that's about 24 sips.

How many people do you know who take a sip of wine after every bite? Observe people enjoying themselves at dinner, as I have, and you cannot help

THE DELICATE FLAVOR OF SUSHI OR SASHIMI MARRIES WELL WITH A LIGHT, DRY CHAMPAGNE.

but notice the typical pattern: several bites of food followed by a sip or two of wine. The actual number of sips of wine taken immediately after a bite of food? Usually no more than five or six per course.

If you follow the Central Premise ("First drink a wine you like") you'll avoid the mistake of choosing a mediocre wine in hopes that it will taste better than it does on its own. Forget mediocre wines. On the other hand, something magical really does happen when the wine and food connect. Those few sips are worth the effort it takes to find a wonderful match.

"The Rules"

The most famous admonition demands white wine with fish and red wine with meat. Other rules command us to drink white wines before red, dry wines before sweet, young wines before old. (One of the new rules that keeps popping up in articles and books is that tart, acidic wines go best with food. Not always. A squeeze of lemon is nice on many things, too, but you can have too much of a good thing.)

Following the rules does not guarantee nirvana, but at least you know dinner won't be awful. The most exciting wine-and-food experiences, however, are the ones that go beyond washing down the food acceptably to create tastes and textures that are new and wonderful.

The real keys

A wine match works by balancing the basic taste of the food, including its texture, with the basic components of wine—sugar, acid, alcohol and tannin. For food, think of the keys as richness and intensity. For wine, think of them as size and weight. The old rule about white wine with fish and red wine with meat comes down to us from the days when white wines were light and red wines were weighty. Today, when many Chardonnays and white Burgundies are heavier and fuller-bodied than most Pinot Noirs and even some Cabernets, color coding does not work so neatly.

With a hearty beef stew, most of us instinctively pass up white wine for red. Why? We're trying to balance the body and intensity of the wine with the same elements in the food. These instincts are right, because the key factor is the delicacy or heartiness of the wine and food, not the color of the wine. Be daring. Try a full-bodied Chardonnay with beef stew. The meat will taste better than it does with most reds.

That bring us to...

The Second Principle

For a comfortable wine-and-food match, the wine should be at least as full-bodied as the food it accompanies.

Hearty food needs a hearty wine, because a lighter wine will fade into the background. With lighter food, you have more leeway. Lighter wines will balance nicely, of course, but heartier wines will still show you all they have. Purists may complain that full-bodied wines "overwhelm" less hearty foods, but the truth is that anything but the blandest food still tastes fine after a sip of a heavyweight wine. Not true the other way around.

Behind the classic matches

Body balancing is the secret of most classic wine-and-food matches. Muscadet washes down a plate of oysters because it's just weighty enough to match the delicacy of a raw bivalve. Cabernet complements grilled lamb chops or roast lamb because they're equally vigorous. Pinot Noir or Burgundy makes a better match with roast beef because the richness of texture is the same in both.

One way to make your own classic matches is to follow the same path as the first person who tried raw oysters with Muscadet. Find a similarly light-bodied wine, such as dry Champagne or a dry Riesling. Don't get stuck on Cabernet with lamb. Try Zinfandel or Côtes du Rhône, which are built along similar lines. Instead of Burgundy or Pinot Noir with roast beef, sample some St.-Émilion or Barbera. That's one way to put a little variety into your wine life without straying too far from the original idea.

Unfortunately, wines do not carry labels listing their weightiness on some widely accepted scale. Most Cabernets are rich and weighty and most Beaujolais are not. Likewise, most Chardonnays are bigger wines than most Champagnes. But not all. Some Burgundies are as delicate as some Beaujolais. Some Chardonnays are steelier and lighter than certain Rieslings.

For this reason, one taste is worth 10 times more than a look at the label. Nothing beats personal experience, but well-written published tasting notes should provide a pretty good idea of where a wine stands on the light-to-heavy scale. Consult the chart below for a quick read on how typical examples of the world's better-known wines fit into this range.

Selected white wines		Selected red wines
Off-dry Riesling (U.S., Australian, German)	**LIGHTEST** ↑ ↓ **HEAVIEST**	Beaujolais
		Dolcetto
Muscadet		Burgundy Côte de Beaune
Dry Riesling (Alsace, U.S.)		
Champagne		Rioja
U.S. Sauvignon Blanc		Chianti Classico
Bordeaux white		California Pinot Noir
Pouilly-Fumé, Sancerre		St.-Émilion, Pomerol
French Chablis (and other unoaked Chardonnays)		Burgundy Côte de Nuits
Mâcon (including Pouilly-Fuissé)		Médoc Classified Growths
Alsace Gewürztraminer		Washington/California Merlot
California barrel-fermented/ barrel-aged Chardonnay		Zinfandel
		California/Washington Cabernet
Meursault, Puligny-Montrachet, Chassagne-Montrachet		Rhône reds, U.S. Syrah, Australian Shiraz
Rhône whites		Barolo

As you can see from the chart, you can choose a red wine with fish or a white wine with beef stew, if you are so inclined, and make a good match. The red wine for fish need only balance the richness and intensity of the dish.

Broiled salmon steak or fresh tuna taste fine with red wines of modest to medium tannins. Rich, full-bodied Chardonnays handle a beef stew with aplomb.

Elements in wine that affect a match

None of wine's attributes is as important as size and weight, but others can help build a bridge or set up a roadblock to the food.

• **Sweetness**. The mere presence of sugar is not enough to affect a match, so long as the wine tastes balanced and not cloying. Anyone who prefers iced tea with sugar should not insist on bone-dry wines. Frankly sweet wines, however, like to find some sweetness in the dish you drink them with, whether it is from fruit, from honey or from almonds. Peppery or spicy foods like a little sweetness in the accompanying wine, too.

• **Tannin**. Many red wines have noticeable tannin, which affects the way a wine feels in the mouth. Certain components in the food can mellow the astringent burr of tannin. Fats and oils tend to neutralize harshness in the wine. So does salt. Think of rich, creamy foods for tannic wines. A chunk of Parmigiano Reggiano cheese is perfect. Beware of foods high in *umami*, however (see below).

• **Alcohol**. Full-bodied wines tend to be high in alcohol, light-bodied wines low. When alcohol is high enough to be noticeable, it can taste a little sweet, which matches well with slightly sweet foods, such as onion-sauced chicken. Very salty food, such as ham, can make high-alcohol wine taste bitter.

• **Temperature**. A much bigger factor than most people realize. Cold temperature tends to mask sweetness and mute flavor. Also, cold emphasizes tannin in red wine. Cold food, muted by temperature, does better with lighter wines, especially if they are also chilled. Think of cold

cuts with Beaujolais or Alsace Gewürztraminer. Spicy food calls for the refreshing texture of a chilled beverage, so if you want to serve wine with spicy food, lean toward chillable ones. If they're a little sweet, so much the better.

• **Acidity**. As a rule, very tart wines taste less acidic when you drink them with food that has an acidic bite itself. Sweet food tends to make acidic wines taste even worse. Very soft wines have trouble matching up to any food, because they tend to wimp out. Drink them by themselves. But as long as the acidity is not the most prominent aspect of the wine, it helps liven the match. After all, many dishes taste fine with a squeeze of lemon.

Umami, the fifth taste

For years I have kept track of why certain foods and wines that should taste great together seem to be touching their thumbs to their noses and waggling their fingers at each other. The missing link, I am convinced, is *umami*. There is no English translation. As noted in chapter 6, the closest might be Brillat-Savarin's "savory taste.". Chinese gourmets have been talking about it for 1,200 years. The concept is not new, but it's only recently gained currency with taste scientists in the west.

Monosodium glutamate triggers the *umami* receptors in your taste buds the same way salt activates the salty receptors and acid zaps the sour buds. To experience a little pure *umami*, dissolve $1/2$ teaspoon of MSG (Accent or Aji-no-moto) in $1/4$ cup of warm water. Taste and spit. *Umami* has a vaguely mushroomy character, to my taste. And, in fact, mushrooms are high in *umami*. So are consommés and long-cooked meats, cured meats, shrimp, dried tomatoes and soy sauce.

Umami's effect on wine

These foods send any bitterness in wine off the charts. That's why foods high in *umami* lay waste to young tannic reds or whites with prominent oak character. I know, for example, that I like to drink Zinfandel with grilled salmon. Even tannic Zins work, because the Zin's tannins melt away next to the salmon's oiliness. I also like sautéed mushrooms with supple Pinot Noirs and Burgundies. I never could figure out why salmon in mushroom sauce clashed with a young Zin. Now I know. The *umami* in the mushrooms emphasizes the tannins in the Zin.

A FULL-BODIED SHIRAZ GOES WELL WITH VENISON AND OTHER GAME.

Young Cabernet matches well with a quick sauté of chicken, the pan deglazed with red wine, chicken broth, shallots and fresh tomatoes. The same ingredients braised slowly make the same young Cabernet taste bitter and metallic. The long-cooking mellows the acidity and bumps up the *umami*. There is a reason why Burgundians choose their older wines for braised beef and chicken. The reduced tannin in older wines doesn't clash with the *umami*. Even if they don't have a word for it, the principles still apply.

Keeping it in perspective

Remember that all of these factors only come into play if they are obvious. A little tomato will not affect a wine match. But a dish that relies on salty ham for its character will dictate which wines will taste best with it. Likewise, a little sweetness won't upset the wine-and-food balance but a lot will.

Like I said before, it's fine-tuning.

The flavor factor

Finally, we come to flavor, for most of us the most enjoyable aspect of the food-and-wine game. Flavors in wine can enhance a dish, just as adding seasoning or extra ingredients does. Once the other aspects of the wine-and-food match are functioning well, flavor nuances can lift the experience onto a loftier plane.

Flavors in the wine can echo those in the food or complement them. An example of echoing the flavors would be a Zinfandel with distinct raspberry flavors served with a duck breast in raspberry sauce. A Chablis with citrus character would complement the flavors of shrimp sautéed in olive oil and garlic by providing the same affect as a squeeze of lemon. You can both echo and complement at the same time. Add dill to the same dish and a tart Sauvignon Blanc with both citrus and herbal flavors would complement the food with its citrus notes and echo the dill flavor with its herbal character.

Pressing the mute button

When you echo a flavor in the food with the wine, the flavor in the food tends to mute the flavor in the wine. I first noticed this phenomenon when drinking an earthy 10-year-old red Burgundy with duck and turnips. The earthy flavor of the turnips canceled out the earthiness in the wine. The unexpected result was that the Burgundy tasted richer in fruit and more youthful, without losing its wonderful sense of maturity. That made for a memorable match.

Savvy wine-and-food matchers can use this information to great advantage. If you're serving a Cabernet Sauvignon with a touch more olive flavor than you care for in wine, add a few sliced olives to the sauce, or make the sauce with olive oil instead of butter. At the table, you can drizzle a little olive oil over the dish. The olive flavors make a bridge between the food and the wine, and they soften the impact of the olive flavor in the wine. Net result: You like the wine even more.

Flavor bridges

The trick is to identify the dominant flavor of the food. It is not necessarily the main ingredient. Often the key flavor is an ingredient added to give the dish its own character. A good example is chicken sauté. Finish the dish with white wine and olives, and the best flavor bridge might be with a Sauvignon Blanc or a Sémillon. But finish it with red wine and mushrooms, and you might think first of Pinot Noir or red Burgundy.

When you see the word "with" in a menu title, chances are the key flavor ingredients comes after the conjunction, not before, as in "monkfish medallions with lemon cream," or "veal chops with wild mushrooms." For a fine-tuned match, the wine's flavors need to address the lemon in the first dish, the wild mushrooms in the second.

Cooking methods can affect the flavor bridge drastically, too. The smoky flavors of grilling or barbecuing tilt the balance in a totally different direction from neutral cooking processes, such as boiling or steaming.

Wine enemies?

Certain foods have a reputation, greatly exaggerated in most cases, for ruining the wine served with them. The important thing to remember about most of these foods is that they are a problem only if they dominate the dish. Just because a sauce contains one of these ingredients doesn't render it an enemy of wine.

Here is a typical enemies list, and some comments:

MANY SALMON DISHES TASTE GREAT WITH PINOT NOIR, A RELATIVELY LIGHT-TEXTURED RED

• **Artichokes**. Artichokes contain a chemical that tends to make anything consumed with them—including water—taste sweet. If artichoke is the main ingredient, then softer, more flavorful wines can clash. If artichoke is just part of the mixture, such as chicken with mushrooms and artichokes or lamb stew with artichokes and other vegetables, just drink a wine with sufficient acidity to compensate for the slight sweetening effect.

• **Garlic**. Who came up with this one? Most cuisines from wine-drinking regions use garlic lavishly. Raw garlic has such strong, aggressive flavor that it can rob a complex wine of its subtleties, but a lively, fruity wine can handle it. What do you think Italians drink with pesto, water? No, a simple white. (Not red; pesto comes from Genoa, and the local wines are mostly whites from the Cinqueterre.)

• **Tomatoes**. Another mystery. Yes, raw tomatoes make a definite flavor statement and nudge the balance of a dish toward acidity, but that's no problem for well-balanced wines. Tomatoes, mozzarella, basil and olive oil make a classic first-course salad. Try it with a crisp white.

• **Anchovies**. Bagna cauda is a Northern Italian dip made mostly of garlic, anchovies and hot olive oil. They dip vegetables into it and drink a fruity red. Complex wines lose

GRILLED QUAIL ACCOMPANIED BY A GLASS OF ZINFANDEL.

their subtlety, of course, but simple, refreshing wines make the grade.

• **Hot peppers**. A light nip of heat from fresh chili peppers bothers few wines of any substance. As the burn quotient rises, however, the best wine choices become increasingly fruitier and sweeter. Try a sweet Chenin Blanc or Vouvray with peppery fish stews, or sweet Sherry with a hot curry.

The real clashers

Excesses of any kind in food can make for a difficult match with wine. Very salty, very peppery or very garlicky dishes narrow the options (although they all can coexist happily with certain wines). The one component in food that can affect wine much more than any of the above is sweetness.

Whether it comes from sweet ingredients such as onions, carrots, beets and fruits or from adding sugar or honey, sweetness in the food affects wine by emphasizing its tannin and acidity. You might like that effect, but most people want their wines to be supple and mellow.

That's why it's best to save the Lafite for some other occasion than Thanksgiving. Most American Thanksgiving tables include not just turkey and gravy but also cranberry sauce, yams with marshmallows and other sweet dishes. Drinking an elegant, dry wine with those foods tends to diminish the wine. Choose simple, fruity wines, even those with a little sweetness, such as a soft Chardonnay or Sauvignon Blanc. Sparkling wines are also a good choice. Red wines should be demonstrably fruity, such as Gamay, Beaujolais, fresh-style Zinfandel or Grenache.

Fresh chestnuts are not nearly as sweet, and if your Thanksgiving table is more wine-savvy—in other words, with nothing sweeter than the chestnuts—you can safely choose almost any dry red or white. In fact, a selection of various wines from white to rosé to red usually makes a crowd happy.

Most Thanksgivings I open a few bottles of four- to five-year-old Zinfandel.

Cooking with wine

Wine marinates meat and poultry, enlivens sauces and stocks, wends its flavor through soups and stews, adds a refreshing note to fruit desserts, and sometimes plays a starring role of its own.

French cooks splash wine into sauté pans to dissolve the browned bits left behind by crisped fish fillets or chicken breasts, producing a ready-made sauce by finishing it with a little butter. Italian cooks pour wine into a bubbling risotto even before they start adding the stock, following the Italian proverb, "Rice lives in water but it dies in wine." Even Chinese cooks use a little Xaoxing (a rice-based wine that closely resembles Sherry) in virtually everything, from marinades to sauces.

Burgundy is famous for its *coq au vin*, a mature chicken stewed in red wine. Alsace, a white wine district, makes *coq au Riesling*. Cooks in Italy's Piedmont district make *risotto con Barolo*, and the traditional Italian dessert, zabaglione, requires Marsala or some similar wine for its distinctive character. Swiss fondue is nothing but cheese melted in white wine, and the classic French sauce *marchand de vin* ("wine merchant's sauce") cooks red wine into a rich brown sauce.

Although these dishes put wine in a starring role, wine usually plays a supporting part in cooking. A touch of its natural acidity can liven up many dishes and balance sauces that would otherwise be excessively rich. Boiled down to a concentrate, wine can add depth to the flavors of a dish.

The three keys to using wine in food are:

1. Use only wines good enough to drink.
2. Cook wine long enough to evaporate most or all of its alcohol.
3. Don't use so much that its acidity throws everything out of whack.

Watch that acidity

Almost every dish that uses wine cooks it long enough to take away its raw taste, which also boils away most of the alcohol. At the same time, other components of the wine become concentrated, especially its natural acids. Recipes that use wine traditionally compensate for this acidity buildup with sweetness in the form of sautéed or caramelized onions, carrots, fruits, liqueurs or natural sweeteners such as honey or sugar. (If you cook with wine, get in the habit of adding a bit of sweetness to any dish with more than a splash of wine—not enough to make the dish sweet, just enough to balance the potential harshness of the wine's acidity.)

Wine acids can cause problems when wine functions as a cooking liquid. Milk or eggs can curdle. Green vegetables toughen or discolor. For such recipes, it is best to add wine at the end of the cooking time. Sometimes the acidity helps, as when wine helps tenderize chicken, duck, beef and lamb, thanks in part to its natural acidity. The acidity in wine helps keep fish firm and fresh. Nothing makes a better poaching liquid for fish than white wine and a little onion.

Always cook with good wine

Cooking with wine concentrates its flavors, which is why fine cooks like to use the best wine possible in their dishes.

All those characteristics connoisseurs prize in a glass of wine can add depth and extra dimensions to food. Fruit flavors top the list, but the vanilla and spice from oak aging add their own personality. So do the herbal, even vegetal, flavors of wines in the Sauvignon family, not to mention the earthiness of Pinot Noirs and mature Syrahs.

How good must a wine be to add the most to a dish? Conventional wisdom is to use at least as good a wine as you would be willing to drink. It need not be expensive or particularly glorious, but if you're opening a good wine for dinner, steal a bit of it to cook into the dish. With older wines, add some of the dregs that are left in the bottle after decanting. Just strain them through a clean towel or a coffee filter.

A little experiment

Cornell University conducted taste tests in the 1970s using three different levels of wine in the same recipes.

For example, the experimenters made a classic French *coq au vin* using a branded "cooking wine," a California Zinfandel and a Chambertin. Then they blind-tasted the food. The Chambertin had a slight edge over the other two wines, but the increment in quality was not great enough to justify the enormous additional cost. Gault et Millau, in their French magazine, conducted a similar test and found that long-cooked dishes tasted best with inexpensive, hearty wines rather than expensive, subtle wines.

Whatever you do, never use a spoiled bottle in cooking. Any off-flavors transfer themselves into the food just as readily as the good flavors.

Wine reductions

One of the best ways to use wine is to boil it with other flavorings (herbs, onions or shallots) to concentrate flavors as the liquid evaporates. This French sauce is a perfect example. The principle is simple: First concentrate the wine with other flavors, which also sharpens the acidity, then soften it with melted butter, which forms an emulsion, as in this classic recipe:

BEURRE BLANC
1/2 cup dry white wine
1 tablespoon white wine vinegar
1 chopped shallot
Pinch of salt and white pepper
Up to 12 tablespoons butter, cut into 12 pats

Put everything except the butter in a nonreactive saucepan (stainless steel or nonstick). Boil the mixture until the liquid reduces in volume to 1 tablespoon. Off heat, start adding the butter, a few pats a time. Swirl the pan to distribute the butter evenly. When one addition of

BEURRE BLANC SAUCE.

butter is almost melted, swirl in a few more pats. Return the pan to low heat for a few seconds at a time to keep it warm, but do not allow it to come close to boiling.

When all the butter is incorporated, taste the sauce for salt and pepper. Strain it if you prefer a smooth sauce. This must be served immediately or kept warm in a Thermos. It will separate if it gets too hot. This recipe makes about 1 1/2 cups.

Use it sparingly on fish or chicken. To make a Beurre Rouge, just substitute red wine. In fact, you can vary this sauce by using different wines (Champagne makes a great alternative) or other flavorings (such as different onions or herbs).

Pre-reducing wine

Because most recipes call for wine to simmer or boil to evaporate the alcohol, a useful trick is to boil the wine first, before adding it to the dish. Then you can be certain that the alcohol has evaporated and no harsh flavors remain. Use a stainless steel or nonstick-lined pan and boil the wine for at least 5 minutes. It should reduce to less than half its original volume. Be careful that the wine that splashes up the sides of the pan does not burn. Stir the wine occasionally, and keep the heat moderate. Add a pinch of sugar or splash of an appropriate liqueur to balance the concentrated acidity. Or leave out the sugar and use the reduced wine in place of vinegar in salad dressings.

Without the alcohol to preserve it, this pre-boiled wine will not keep long. Use it the same day or keep it in the refrigerator for up to two days.

Better yet, freeze it in an ice cube tray. When it is frozen, pop the cubes into a plastic freezer bag. Anytime a recipe calls for wine, just add the right number of cubes and save the step of boiling down the wine. The cubes keep for six to nine months.

Deglazing pans

After roasting or sautéing meat, fish or poultry, the pan contains coagulated flavor in the form of drippings or browned bits stuck to the bottom. Pour off the fat and use a splash of wine to dissolve that flavor into a sauce.

Put the pan over moderate heat. Add about $1/2$ cup of wine (precision is not necessary). It will sizzle and steam. Use a spatula to scrape up the browned bits until they dissolve. Add this flavor concentrate to your sauce.

Or make a quick sauce right in the pan. Add a spoonful of chopped shallots or onions along with the wine. When the browned bits are scraped up, add a cup or two of basic white or brown sauce, tomato sauce, or just a little melted butter, and simmer for a minute or two.

The Essence

The price of wine reflects what the market will bear, not necessarily how much it costs to produce. Prices also vary depending on where you buy the wine. In most restaurants, for example, expect to pay double (or more) what you would for the same wine in a retail shop.

A bottle of wine goes through a series of hands as it gets to you from the winery. At each step, mishandling can compromise the wine's quality. Always taste a bottle before buying a whole case if you're unsure about it. Use wine merchants who can consistently deliver well-maintained wines.

Acquire hard-to-find wines by developing a friendly relationship with a retailer who can order them for you. You can also seek out wines through secondary channels, such as buying at auction after the wine has been in circulation for a few years, or haunting out-of-the-way wine shops for forgotten bottles and cases.

CHAPTER TWELVE

The Business of Wine,

or, How to Be a Savvy Wine Consumer

Much as we like to think of wine as an artistic expression, the people who produce it must think of it as a business. If they don't, they cannot afford to keep making it. After all, there is no National Endowment for the Wine Arts. If it doesn't sell, it doesn't get made. To sell it, the wine industry employs production and marketing techniques every bit as sophisticated as any other commercial enterprise. Why, for example, does one wine cost $100 while another, which looks remarkably similar—and might even taste as good or better—costs $10? Why does the same wine cost $8 in a big chain store, $10 in a fine wine shop and $25 in a restaurant? How can one bottle purchased in Store A taste so much better than an identically labeled bottle from Store B? Why can you seldom seem to find the hot new wines that your wine-savvy friends are talking about?

This chapter answers those questions and more, and offers a guide to being a savvy consumer. If we wine buyers are to make wise decisions about the thousands of wine choices out there, it helps to understand the rudiments of the business.

The Ouch Factor

Some years ago, a winemaker showed me a series of charts that demonstrated how much it actually costs to make a bottle of wine. He added up the investments in planting, managing and harvesting a vineyard; building a winery and all its equipment; buying barrels, bottles, corks, labels and boxes; paying winemakers and staff. It was enough to convince me that no one can ever make a profit producing wine. Then I saw the winemaker and a lot of his colleagues driving around in their BMWs, and I realized that something was out of whack.

The X Factor is marketing. It's about creating an image and persuading consumers that the wine is worth whatever the winemaker suggests. If the market responds, then the price goes up. And up. And up. That is what happened in the 1990s. The wine market became competitive, but the competition was among buyers—that's you and me—to buy the wines we wanted.

When I first started writing about wine, Heitz Cabernet Sauvignon Martha's Vineyard was the most expensive wine in California. I think it cost $10 when other good Cabs were selling for $6. I asked Joe Heitz how he arrived at $10. "I keep raising the price until they say ouch, then I stop," he responded. That, in a pungent and revealing phrase, is how wine prices are set throughout most of the world.

What happens if the wine doesn't sell at the high price?

If the winery overshoots the mark and can't sell all of its wine at the listed price, you might think that the reasonable response would be to lower the price. But a winery dreads lowering its price because that would imply that the wine is not as terrific as all the marketing literature claims. Instead, here's what happens. It continues to sell as much of the wine as it can at the high price, and sells the rest under another name, usually at a reduced price. It might sell it in bulk to a big winery, which may bottle it separately or use it to beef up a blend. Or, more often, the winery may sell it as a private-label wine to a restaurant or hotel.

Either way, the price on the winery's own label remains high, which preserves its marketing niche. But if you know where the wine ended up, you can enjoy it for less. How do you find out? The retailer or a restaurateur who ended up with the wine might suggest it to you. They're not supposed to know where the wine came from, and if they do they're not supposed to tell, but if they sense you know your stuff they'll probably tip you off.

How wine gets from the winery to you

Once the winery bottles and packs the wine, it follows a long and winding road to your dinner table. A typical bottle of Bordeaux, for example, leaves the cellar in the hands of a courtier—the middleman who moves the wine from the château to the shipper's storehouse. Then it travels on another truck to a shipping point, where it is transferred to a boat or airplane. Upon arrival in the U.S., our Bordeaux is handed off from the importer to a distributor, who delivers it to the retail shop or restaurant, who then delivers it to you. At any stage there can also be intermediate stops.

Each step adds to the cost of the bottle, but worse, each step is one more opportunity for something to go wrong. The biggest bugaboo is temperature. The elite shippers often use refrigerated containers, but others prefer to save money by shipping wine in so-called dry boxes in spring or fall, when they are not likely to encounter the full heat of summer. Properly handled, the wine does not suffer in transit, but the truth is we don't know what the temperature was when the wine was shipped from the winemaker to the distributor, or in the distributors' warehouses, or in the truck from the distributor to the retailer, or in the retail store itself. Rare is the store where the temperature is kept at a chilly 55° to 60° F 24 hours a day.

A GOOD WINE MERCHANT WILL TAKE TIME TO LEARN YOUR TASTES AND SUGGEST WINES YOU MIGHT ENJOY.

This is the dirty little

secret of the wine business. Importers, distributors and retailers assure us that they ship and store wine at the proper temperatures, but in several investigations in the past 10 years, *Wine Spectator* editors have discovered that this is not always so. Exposure for a few days or weeks to 70° to 80° temperatures is not going to ruin a wine—although it will accelerate the aging process. The problem comes when cases of wine languish in hot (100°F) warehouses, or in the steamy holds of ships traversing the Panama Canal during a heat wave. Under these conditions, wine should be shipped in refrigerated containers.

Although most wine gets to reputable stores through reputable channels, a significant percentage does not, and no one knows how much. Some big names honor these concerns only in the breach. A container of wine can be left to simmer on a hot New Jersey dock in August, rapidly robbing the wine of its flavor, or it can freeze in an uninsulated truck crossing the Rocky Mountains in December, which can push out corks as the wine expands.

The best thing to do is taste a bottle of any wine you question, either at the store before you buy it (if the proprietor has a bottle opened for sampling) or by opening a case at home and trying a bottle within a few weeks to make sure it doesn't taste prematurely old. If it's not what it should be, contact the retailer and explain the problem. It's easier to deal with these things right away than after the wine has aged for several years.

Who to trust

Let's start with the premise that most people who sell wine try to do an honest job. After all, there is no percentage in scamming a customer who might come back and buy several hundred dollars' worth of additional wine. Intentionally or not, however, stores and wine salesmen can mislead.

Beware of the know-it-all wine salesman, for example, who is full of "inside" information. I remember one salesman who insisted to me that a winery I knew to be privately owned was a label invented by Gallo. A good salesman spends time ascertaining your tastes so he can suggest an appropriate wine. If he seems more intent on displaying his own supposed knowledge, treat his suggestions with the respect they deserve.

Two ways to beat the system

Where state laws permit it, anyone can set up his own import business, a procedure called direct importing. It requires buying a license and paying the appropriate taxes, but it can be worth it for serious collectors investing thousands of dollars in wines that they know have been handled properly, and with a minimum number of transfers, from the winery's cellar door to theirs. (In practice, most direct importers are retailers and restaurateurs who want to get their hands on wines that are not always available through regular channels.)

Then there is the gray market. Normally, producers and importers work together to create a market that will maximize everyone's return, which usually means getting the wine to the most people in good condition. Along the way, allocations are made (meaning so much wine goes to one wholesale customer, so much to another). Entrepreneurial importers can do an end run around these allocations, particularly with wines that are in great demand, such as classified-growth Bordeaux and top-name Burgundy, by buying the wine from merchants elsewhere in France or in third countries.

The gray market can provide hard-to-find wines and even offer them at a bargain. But if anything, the wine must pass through even more hands than it would going through normal channels. I've had perfectly fine gray market wines, and perfectly disappointing bottles. Caveat emptor.

Should you stock up at the winery?

If you live near the source, you can of course buy at the winery and skip all the middlemen. Residents of the U.K. buy wine on vacation in France and Italy, for instance, and take it back home all the time. That makes sense in Europe because small wineries usually sell at the same price to consumers as they do to restaurateurs, retailers and exporters, who in turn can take whatever markup they like. Although bigger customers will get discounts, the price you pay at a French, Spanish or Italian winery will still probably be less than what you can find in a store on either side of the Atlantic.

When a U.S. winery sells direct from its tasting room or via mail order, though, it acts as producer, distributor and retailer—all in one. You would think the wine would cost you less, but most of the time you'll pay the full retail price. Most wineries want to sell their wines at retail elsewhere. Rather than offend the big buyers and sellers, wineries keep their tasting room prices at full markup.

There are good reasons to buy wine at a winery, however. Sometimes you can buy small-lot wines and special bottlings that never get into wide distribution. Even if you buy a wine that you could have bought at a local shop, you'll relive your visit when you open it. Besides, it's good form to buy a bottle or two after the proprietor has poured you several tastes.

The winery tasting room and tour

Visiting wine country adds extra dimensions to your enjoyment of wine. It makes connections in your memory between the wines, the places they come from and the people who make them. Use the experience to learn as much as you can about how the wine was produced. See the vineyards if you can. Get the lay of the land. Feel how one region might be different from the next. Meet the people and let them tell you how they make their wines. Every story is a little different, every winery reflects a different atti-

THE OPUS ONE WINERY IN OAKVILLE, NAPA VALLEY.

tude and understanding of what wine is and how it should fit into life.

Alas, the hordes that descend upon Napa Valley and other tourist-centric wine regions mostly want to soak up as much fermented grape juice as they can. To discourage profligate boozing, most wineries have instituted such practices as requiring a tour before tasting, charging per taste, or requiring you to buy a glass. Often these charges are deducted from the purchase price of a bottle.

This is all to the good, especially for those who visit wine country on rare occasions. After the fifth or sixth winery tour, they all kind of blend together—not because of excess wine consumption but because, frankly, most wineries pretty much look alike behind the exterior architecture. They have a crush pad, a tank room, a barrel room, a bottling line, a cellar or cooled warehouse for storage.

If you've never seen the inside of a winery, however, do take a few tours. It will help you to understand the wine-making process. Besides, it's cooler inside than it is outdoors during the summer.

Tips for visiting wine country

- Wineries come in all shapes and sizes. Plan to visit a variety of wineries—some big, some small.

- Smaller wineries usually require an appointment for tours. Write, fax or e-mail in advance. They want to see you. They just don't want to be inundated with big crowds.

- With that in mind, concentrate on wineries whose wines you have liked and want to learn more about.

- If you're new to wine country, start with at least one winery with a comprehensive tour that offers experienced tour guides or illustrative plaques or posters to show you the winemaking process. In Napa Valley, that list would include Robert Mondavi, Beringer, Sterling, St. Supery, Domaine Mumm and Domaine Chandon.

- Only serious professionals should schedule more than three or four winery visits a day. Designate a driver who must spit, not swallow, the tastes. Or hire a car and driver.

- Ask questions. It's the best way to learn.

When wine is released

In an old commercial for Paul Masson winery, Orson Welles intoned, "We will sell no wine before its time." The joke among startup wineries is that their banks say when "it's time." It's when the payment is due on the loan.

In Europe, appellation laws stipulate the earliest date that a wine can be released. In general, white wine is ready sooner than red; most regions get their basic whites out within a year, reds within two. Wine labeled reserve, reserva or riserva must age a year or two longer than those with no such designations.

Bordeaux follows a unique pattern, generally shipping its wines two years after the vintage. However, it offers futures—contracts for a certain amount of wine at a certain price— to the trade in the spring immediately following the vintage, while the wines are still in cask. Generally, the châteaus offer up to one-third of the wine in this form as a means of setting the price for the vintage and generating some cash flow. These futures are then resold up the line; a significant number of them are always offered by retailers to consumers. From the consumer's point of view, buying futures is a way of guaranteeing a supply of the wine, even though it will not be delivered for two years or more. It can also be a bargain. In a good vintage, prices can double from first offering to final release. In some vintages, however, prices remain steady. Usually it's somewhere in between.

Until recently, the only wine futures were offerings by Bordeaux châteaus. Other wineries in other regions have picked up on the idea, offering pre-sale prices on their wines.

Consumers must buy these futures from retailers. This system is not as volatile as Bordeaux's organized stock market-like trade, but it does give consumers a chance to reserve bottles of some of their favorite collectibles, particularly those from California (mostly Cabernet Sauvignon), Burgundy, Rhône, Piedmont and Tuscany. However, buying pre-release wines ties up your money, often long before you have a chance to taste the wine and decide whether you really like it. It works best for blue-chip wines that are in such demand that you can later change your mind and sell them, provided you can do it legally (or without getting caught).

In the New World, no regulations require that wine be sold at any given time. As a result, wineries can release wine whenever it makes sense for them. This creates a moving target for collectors and wine writers who want to know how good a particular vintage is and which wines are worth buying from it. For any given vintage, the wines come onto the market over a span of two years for Chardonnays and up to four years for Cabernets. At any given time, store shelves are full of newly released wines from three or four vintages.

Unless you're obsessed with compulsively collecting only the best of the best (in which case this book probably isn't for you, anyway), my advice is just to find wines you like and buy them. There's plenty out there to choose from.

Labels and bottles: the design and the message

Labels are like album covers on musical recordings. Aside from delivering the basic information required to identify the contents, they project an image.

Some wineries commission art specific for a particular wine or even a particular vintage. Château Mouton-Rothschild started a trend when it commissioned world-famous artists to create a new work for each vintage of its wine. (It saved Picasso for the year it officially became a first growth, 1973, which unfortunately was not a great, long-lived vintage.) Today, wineries all over the world emulate the practice, commissioning artists to create something unique for specific vintages.

Some keep it simple, implying elegance and aristocracy with clean, unadorned typography. Others jazz it up, using colors and shapes to create a fun look. From a marketing standpoint, the goal of any wine label is to stand out from the crowd on the shelf. As consumers, we must be aware of the psychological pull of packaging.

Ultimately, of course, buying a wine by the label makes as much sense as picking a racehorse by its colors, but I know some sensitive souls who won't buy a wine with a label they consider ugly. "I won't have that label on my table," they say. "Use a decanter," I respond.

Decoding a back label

Not all wines have back labels. No law requires them, but, particularly in the New World, wineries take advantage of the chance to explain their wines a little more and do a little public relations for the winery. Some go no further, slapping the same generic our-winery-is-so-great story on every wine they make.

The most useful labels tell you something about the wine that the front label does not, such as describing something about the vineyard or winemaking that distinguishes the wine, the varietal composition, barrel-aging regime, sugar content or the style the winemaker tried to achieve. I also like back labels that entertain with either humor or good descriptive writing.

For a while there in the 1970s and 1980s, it seemed as if every winemaker had to provide a technical report on the back label, listing the degrees brix at which the grapes were picked and the pH of the must. That era has passed, but many back labels couch potentially useful information in techno-speak. Here is a brief decoder:

• Brix is the sugar percentage of the grapes on a 100-point scale. In a dry wine, all the sugar converts to alcohol, so a

Tales of Le Sophiste
(1993: Roussanne 92.1%, Marsanne 7.9%)
Santa Cruz Mountains

Sophism: from Gk. *sophistes* sage (def.):
A specious argument for displaying
ingenuity in reasoning or for deceiving
someone. Oh beautiful for specious
skies. The original Sophists (who did not
share the Platonic view) are misunder-
stood today, as it was Plato who wrote
their history. They were sage but not
disingenuous or jaded and perhaps were
the first true Empiricists. They com-
mented on what they could see, touch,
hear, taste and smell. True sophistication
is timeless, not particularly *à la mode*.
Though they are but *arrivistes*,
Marsanne and Roussanne
belong in the Santa Cruz Mts.,
specifically in a small hamlet called
Bonny Doon. Here they marry to produce
a unique wine of distinction, puissant
and fragrant, that will delight
even the untutored *naïf*. This
wine has not been filtered.

14.4% ALC. BY VOLUME
PRODUCED AND BOTTLED BY
BONNY DOON VINEYARD SANTA CRUZ, CA. U.S.A.

LE SOPHISTE

BONNY DOON IS FAMOUS FOR
ITS UNIQUE AND HUMOROUS
LABELS.

high number (for most wines above 23 degrees) suggests a riper, fuller-bodied wine.

• Labels that quote figures for acidity are usually meaning-less, because they seldom mention it at all if the acidity is particularly low or high.

• Barrel-fermented or barrel-aged wines may refer to the type of barrel used, usually by the country or forest of origin. If you know the taste of wine aged in Tronçais oak as opposed to Nevers oak, this can be useful. If the label bothers to mention it, the winery spent a lot of money on the barrels and wants you to know it. That's the message.

• Labels that don't use the word "barrel" but just say "oak" can phrase it that way because they didn't put the wine in barrels at all but aged it in a tank with oak chips. It's a per-fectly nice way to add a touch of oak flavor to a simple wine, but provides none of the other benefits of aging wine in small oak barrels.

Removing and saving labels

A lot of people like to collect wine labels from bottles they've enjoyed and preserve them in a scrapbook or photo album. Usually, immersing the bottle in warm water does the trick. If not, try adding one part ammonia cleaner to eight parts of hot water, making sure the area you're working in is well-ventilated. (Breathing ammonia is nasty.) Once the labels are dry, use an iron to flatten out any bumps and puckers.

Some adhesives don't seem to want to loosen up for anything. If ammonia doesn't work, try citric acid (otherwise known as "sour salt") dissolved in warm water. This works better on the new pressure-sensitive adhesives.

How to acquire hard-to-find wines

Reputable auction houses try to ensure the rare wines they sell have been properly stored, but wine that's gone bad is not returnable.

Because the market is large and supplies are limited, there are no guarantees that any specific bottle will be available in a given market. Wineries don't always know where their products end up, and while there are many mail-order companies, local laws may prohibit buying from them. The best tack is to develop a friendly relationship with a good local retailer who can order the wines you want.

One way to unearth some wine treasures is to haunt liquor stores in out-of-the-way places, where they may not realize what they have. Sometimes you can find single-vineyard bottlings price-tagged below the regular bottling. But take careful note of storage conditions. In most stores with air conditioning, the temperatures are probably about 65°F at night to 72°F in the summer daytime, and if the bottles are kept on their sides and not exposed to direct light, they could be worth buying and opening soon to see how they are progressing. If the wines have been kept out on the store shelves under adverse conditions, I would be wary of spending much money on them. Several years of 70-degree temperatures alone would make me say, "no thanks." However, if the wines had been stored in a cool cellar and only recently been brought to the sales floor, they might be good buys. Ask.

Buying and trading older wine

After several years, desirable wines often appear on the resale market. Buying at auction is one way to acquire hard-to-find wines.

Anyone can buy or sell mature, drinkable bottles legally at auction. *Wine Spectator* tracks the prices of key blue-chip wines and publishes updates several times a year on its auction page. Up-to-date information is also available on the *Wine Spectator* Web site at www.winespectator.com.

Individuals cannot sell wine legally in most states, which puts the brakes on a great deal of wine speculation. On the other hand, private transactions between friends rarely attract legal scrutiny. Many collectors take the risk. In some states, retailers can legally buy and sell wine from consumers.

The key to buying good bottles of these older wines is provenance—which is to say, the history of the actual bottles being offered for sale. Where have they been stored? Under what conditions? Most auction catalogs list only where the wine was stored just prior to that sale. Reputable auction houses such as Sotheby's, Christie's, Chicago Wine Co., and Butterfield & Butterfield try to ensure good provenance for the wines they sell, but you can't return a bottle if it's corky or gone bad in some other way.

Retailers often get their older wines on consignment from collectors, so they know the provenance of the wines better than auction houses, but few retailers can match the breadth of wines offered at auction.

Learning more: wine online

The Internet can be a tremendous wine information resource. More and more wineries are putting up Web sites where you can learn about their wines and activities. Retail shops offer access to their catalogues. You can exchange comments in Internet newsgroups, and with discussion groups on many Web sites and on subscription services such as America Online, CompuServe and Prodigy. Wine research is available at university Web sites. Regional information is available from promotional and trade organizations. Wine lovers of all stripes—and levels of expertise—offer their own Web sites.

A good way to start, of course, is at *Wine Spectator*'s own Web site (www.winespectator.com). It offers new material daily, plus archives of tasting notes and past articles from the publication, databases of wine-and-food matches, hotels and restaurants, and lots more.

To look for more on the Internet, use one of the big portals. My favorites include Snap!, Yahoo, Excite, Alta Vista and Dogpile. Just enter the word "wine" in the search blank and start surfing. Or enter a specific wine region, winery or wine type, and see what comes up. You'll be amazed at what's out there.

A few sites actually sell wine over the Internet. In the U.S., you can only buy wine legally in the same state where you live or from a state with which your state has made a reciprocal agreement. Some wine sellers on the Web use distributors in each state so they can sell anywhere in the U.S. As with any purchases you might make on the Web, check out whoever you're buying from to make sure they're legit.

Some final words: ten myths about wine

We explored some of these in greater depth elsewhere, but they're worth repeating because you're certain to hear someone voice any or all of them as incontrovertible fact.

1. Cheap wines are never any good. Usually expressed by a snob—the classic "label drinker"—who only buys and drinks wines that have some sort of official reputation. The truth is that there are plenty of inexpensive wines that are much better than their prices suggest. They come from producers or regions that have not yet established big reputations, or they are made from grape varieties that are currently out of fashion, such as Riesling.

2. Expensive wines are not worth it. This is reverse snobbery, uttered by those who can't imagine why anyone would pay that much for wine (or a hotel room, or an opera ticket, or a car...) My motto: drink the best you can afford to buy.

3. New World wines are never as good as French wines. Long disproved, but an idea that just won't go away.

4. Traditional winemaking is the only way to make fine wine. More controversial, but also without merit. How do you define "traditional"? Ideas of how things should be done evolve, and what is now considered traditional was once radical. Bad modern winemaking cuts corners and cheapens the final product. Good modern winemaking understands why traditional methods work and tries to achieve the same goal or improve upon it. How can anyone quarrel with that?

5. Ratings favor power over finesse. True only to the extent that all great wines exhibit distinctive and concentrated flavors, but good tasters also seek finesse and elegance before they award a high rating to a wine. That said, do not ignore moderately rated wines, because they can offer charm as opposed to intensity. Good music is not always loud.

6. Panel tastings flatten scores so no wines stand out. This depends on the process. If you just average everyone's ratings, then the most distinctive wines can be penalized when some tasters love them and others hate them. If there is some discussion before arriving at a final ranking, then very distinctive wines have a better chance. Either way, panel tastings tend to reward the wines most likely to appeal to the greatest number of wine drinkers.

7. Breathing is always good for wine. Some wines are best as soon as the cork comes out. This is especially so for older wines. Others improve after exposure to air. A few are even better the next day. Which ones will behave which way? Who knows? Pour the wine into a glass and find out.

8. Old wine is better. I must admit that the very greatest wines I have ever drunk were wines that had aged for years in perfect cellar conditions. But some of my most disappointing wines have come out of the same cellars. Only a tiny percentage of the world's wines gets better with age. Unless a wine has a long track record of aging well, cellaring it for more than a couple of years is a risk. The rewards can be great, but the odds get longer with each passing year.

9. There is only one perfect wine for every dish. This one would drive you nuts if it were true. But it is no more true than saying that there is only one perfect dish for every wine. Fortunately, many wines match up nicely with most dishes, and vice versa. Some combinations do better than others, to be sure, and much of the fun lies in discovering the winning combos.

10. Beginning wine drinkers start by liking sweet wines and learning to drink dry wines. Often true, but not always. Do you like your iced tea unsweetened? Then you'll probably like dry wines. Do you add a couple of sugar packets? Better start with sweet wines.

Glossary

This glossary defines terms you are likely to encounter in wine conversations or on wine labels. It includes some wine-tasting terms, but not words that refer to specific fruits, vegetables or minerals. (It's pretty obvious that "raisiny" means that something in the wine smells and tastes like raisins.)

ACETIC ACID: The component in wine that can make it taste like vinegar. All wines contain some acetic acid but usually the amount is not perceptible. A little can enhance the character of a wine, but when it becomes the dominant flavor, it is a major flaw. See also ETHYL ACETATE.

ACID, ACIDITY: The grape contributes a variety of acids to the finished wine, including tartaric, malic, lactic and citric. In balance, acid adds crispness and brightness to enliven and shape flavors, and helps prolong the aftertaste. A good thing, in moderation, but not when it makes the wine taste sour.

AERATION: Exposing wine to air, either by decanting the bottle into another container or by simply pouring the wine into a glass and swirling it around. Many wines seem to gain more softness and flavor over several minutes to several hours before starting to fade. Very old wines just start to fade. Also called BREATHING.

AGGRESSIVE: Tasting term for unpleasantly harsh in taste or texture, usually due to a high level of tannin or acid.

ALCOHOL: Ethyl alcohol, a chemical compound formed when natural or added yeast consumes the grapes' sugar during fermentation.

ALCOHOL BY VOLUME: The law requires wine labels to state the alcohol content, usually expressed as a percentage of volume. For table wines the law allows a 1.5 percent variation above or below the stated percentage as long as the alcohol does not exceed 14 percent. Wines labeled as "table wine" fall into the 11 to 14 percent range.

ALLIER: Pronounced *ahl-yaih*, a forest in France that produces oak used for barrels. See also FRENCH OAK.

AMERICAN OAK: Marked by strong vanilla, dill or cedar aromas, American oak is used extensively for aging Zinfandel, Merlot and Cabernet. It's less desirable for Chardonnay or Pinot Noir. Wineries in California, Spain and Australia use American oak. See also FRENCH OAK.

AMERICAN VITICULTURAL AREA (AVA): A delimited, geographical grape-growing area that has officially been given appellation status by the Bureau of Alcohol, Tobacco and Firearms. Two examples are Napa Valley and Willamette Valley. See also VITICULTURAL AREA.

AMPELOGRAPHY: The study of grape varieties.

APPELLATION: Defines a wine by naming the area where the grapes were grown for it, such as Bordeaux, Chianti, Alexander Valley or Russian River Valley. See also APPELLATION D'ORIGINE CONTROLEE, AMERICAN VITICULTURAL AREA, D.O.C., GEOGRAPHICAL INDICATION.

APPELLATION D'ORIGINE CONTROLEE (AOC): The French system of appellations,

begun in the 1930s and considered the wine world's prototype. To carry an appellation in this system, a wine must follow rules describing the area the grapes are grown in, the varieties used, the ripeness, the alcoholic strength, the vineyard yields and the methods used in growing the grapes and making the wine.

AROMA: Purists define it as the smell that wine acquires from the grapes. Now it more commonly means the wine's total smell, including changes that result from fermentation and oak aging or bottle aging. See also BOUQUET.

ASTRINGENT: An excessively rough, drying, puckery texture, usually from tannin.

AUSTERE: Tasting term for a wine that lacks roundness. Usually said of young wines that need time to soften, or wines that lack richness and body.

AWKWARD: Tasting term for a wine that has poor structure or feels out of balance.

BACKBONE: Tasting term for noticeable acidity, alcohol and tannin in balance.

BACKWARD: Tasting term for a young wine, less developed than others of its type and class from the same vintage.

BALTHAZAR: An oversized bottle which holds the equivalent of 12 to 16 standard bottles.

BARREL FERMENTED: Indicates wine that has been fermented in small casks (usually 55-gallon oak barrels) instead of larger tanks, used mainly for whites.

BIN NUMBER: A means of identifying a separate lot of wine. It has no legal definition.

BITE: Tasting term for marked acidity or tannin.

BLANC DE BLANCS: "White of whites," meaning a white wine made of white grapes, such as Champagne made of Chardonnay.

BLANC DE NOIRS: "White of blacks," white wine made of red or black grapes. The juice is squeezed from the grapes and fermented without picking up much color from the skins, as in Champagne made from Pinot Noir and Pinot Meunier.

BODY: Tasting term for the impression of weight or fullness on the palate, usually the result of a combination of alcohol and sugar. Commonly expressed as full-bodied, medium-bodied or medium-weight, or light-bodied.

BOTRYTIS CINEREA: A mold or fungus that attacks grapes under moist climatic conditions and causes them to shrivel, concentrating flavor, sugar and acid. Some of the most famous examples come from Sauternes, Germany and Hungary. Also known as *pourriture noble* (French), *edelfäule* (German), and "noble rot."

BOTTLE SICKNESS: Wines that have just been moved or shipped often seem muted or have disjointed fruit flavors. Also called bottle shock. A few days of rest is the cure.

BOTTLED BY: When not preceded by "produced by," means that the brand owner did not ferment the wine in its own winery but either bought it in bulk or contracted with another winery to make it.

BOUQUET: Technically the smell that develops from fermentation and aging, though it is commonly used as a synonym for AROMA.

CELLARED BY: On U.S. labels, means none of the wine was produced at the winery where it was bottled. It usually indicates that the wine was purchased from another source.

CHAPTALIZATION: The addition of sugar to juice before and/or during fermentation, originally used to boost sugar levels in underripe grapes and alcohol levels in the subsequent wines but also used to prolong fermentation in Burgundy.

CHARMAT: Mass production method for sparkling wine in which the wines undergo secondary fermentation in large stainless steel tanks and are bottled under pressure. Also known as the "bulk process." See also MÉTHODE CHAMPENOISE.

CHEWY: Tasting term for rich, heavy, tannic wines. Not a fault in young, ageable wines.

CIGAR BOX: Another descriptor for a cedary aroma, often with a tobacco note.

CLEAN: Tasting term for a wine free of any off tastes. Does not necessarily imply good quality.

CLONE: A vine originating from a single, individual plant propagated asexually from a single source. Clones are selected for their unique qualities, such as flavor, productivity and adaptability to growing conditions.

CLOSED: Tasting term for wines that are concentrated and have character, yet are shy in aroma or flavor.

CLOUDINESS: Lack of clarity to the eye. Acceptable for old wines with sediment, but in younger wines it can signal protein instability, yeast spoilage or re-fermentation in the bottle.

COARSE: Tasting term usually referring to texture, and in particular, excessive tannin or oak. Also used

BREATHING: See AERATION.

BRIGHT: Tasting term for fresh, ripe, zesty young wines with vivid flavors.

BRILLIANT: Tasting term for very clear wines with absolutely no visible suspended or particulate matter. Not always a plus, as it can indicate a highly filtered wine.

BRIX: A measurement of the sugar content of grapes, must and wine expressed as the percentage of sugar in the liquid. Most table-wine grapes are harvested at between 21 and 25 Brix, which ferments to 12 to 14 percent alcohol.

BROWNING: If a wine's color starts to brown, it is a sign that a wine is mature. A bad sign in young red (or white) wines, but less significant in older wines.

BRUT: Designation for a relatively dry-finished Champagne or sparkling wine, often the driest wine made by the producer.

BURNT: Tasting term for an overdone, smoky, toasty or singed character.

BUTTERY: Tasting term for the smell or texture of melted butter or toasty oak, as in "a rich, buttery Chardonnay."

CARBONIC MACERATION: Fermenting whole, uncrushed grapes in a carbon dioxide atmosphere, which results in ebulliently fruity and floral flavors, early drinkability and short-lived wine.

CASK NUMBER: See BIN NUMBER.

CEDARY: Tasting term for the smell of cedar wood common in Cabernet Sauvignon and Cabernet blends aged in oak.

to describe harsh bubbles in sparkling wines.

COLD STABILIZATION: A clarification technique in which a wine's temperature is lowered to near freezing, causing tartrates and other solids to precipitate so they can be removed.

COMPLEXITY: Tasting term for a desirable combination of many flavors along with depth, intensity and balance.

CORKY: Tasting term for the musty, moldy-newspaper flavor and aroma and drying aftertaste caused by a tainted cork. Also known as CORKED.

CRU CLASSÉ: French, literally "classed site," used on Bordeaux labels for vineyards officially ranked in the top tiers.

CRUSH: Harvest season, when the grapes are picked and crushed for fermentation.

CUVÉE: A blend or special lot of wine.

DECANTING: A process for separating the sediment from a wine before drinking. Accomplished by letting the sediment settle to the bottom of a bottle, then slowly and carefully pouring the wine into another container, leaving the sediment behind.

DELICATE: Tasting term for light-to medium-weight wines with appealing flavors. A desirable quality in wines such as Pinot Noir or Riesling.

DEMI-SEC: Literally "half dry." Sparkling wines carrying this designation are noticeably sweet.

DENSE: Tasting term for concentrated aromas and flavors. A good sign in young wines.

DEPTH: Tasting term for the concentration and complexity of flavors.

DIRTY: Covers any and all foul, rank, off-putting smells that can occur in a wine.

D.O.C. Denominazione d'Origine Controllata, the Italian system for defining wine regions and wine names. D.O.C.G. (... e Garantita) covers regions willing to submit their wines to tougher requirements, including tasting approval.

DOSAGE: Pronounced doe-SAZH. In bottle-fermented sparkling wines, a small amount of wine (usually sweet) that is added back to the bottle once the yeast sediment that collects in the neck of the bottle is removed.

DRY: Having no perceptible taste of sugar. Most wine tasters begin to perceive sugar at levels of 0.3 percent to 0.7 percent. Some labels apply the term to wines with as much as 2 percent residual sugar.

DRYING OUT: Tasting term for losing fruit (or sweetness in sweet wines) to the extent that acid or tannin dominate the taste. An irreversible process.

DUMB: Tasting term for a phase in young wines when their initial freshness has faded and bottle character has not yet developed. Same as CLOSED.

EARTHY: Tasting term for a character reminiscent of the clean smell of wet earth (if meant as a positive) or overly funky, barnyardy odors (if meant as a negative). You can tell which by the context.

ELEGANT: Tasting term for wines in which all the elements mesh gracefully.

ENOLOGY: The science and study of winemaking. Also spelled oenology.

ESTATE-BOTTLED: On American wine labels, it indicates that the

grapes for the wine came from the winery's own vineyard or one it controls with a long-term lease, and in the same viticultural area.

ETHYL ACETATE: A chemical produced in fermentation that smells like nail polish remover; usually occurs in conjunction with ACETIC ACID. In small doses it can enhance fruit flavors. When it is obvious, it's a defect.

EXTRA-DRY: Confusingly, on sparkling wine labels it means the wine is sweet.

EXTRACT: Italian enologists actually bake a sample of wine and measure the dry residue to determine extract. As a tasting term, it refers to richness and concentration of fruit flavors.

FAT: Full-bodied, high alcohol wines low in acidity give a "fat" impression on the palate. Desirable if flavors are bold and ripe, a fault if the structure is suspect. See also FLABBY

FERMENTATION: The process by which yeast turns grape juice into wine by converting sugar into alcohol and carbon dioxide.

FIELD BLEND: When several different varieties grow side by side in the same vineyard and are harvested and vinified together to produce a single wine.

FILTERING: Pumping wine or must through a screen or pad to remove particles from it. Most wines are filtered for both clarity and stability. Overly severe filtration can also strip flavor.

FINESSE: Most wine tasters use it to mean "fine-ness," but I like the dictionary's definition of "artful delicacy." When a big wine manages to be subtle, or when a delicate wine delivers big flavor, that's finesse.

FINING: A technique for clarifying wine in tank or cask using agents such as bentonite (powdered clay), gelatin or egg whites, which combine with sediment and settle to the bottom, where they can be easily removed.

FINISH: A tasting term for a wine's final impression left in the mouth; also called aftertaste. A good finish lasts. Great wines have rich, long, complex finishes. See also LENGTH

FIRM: Tasting term meaning having enough tannin and acidity to be felt without their overpowering the wine.

FLABBY: Beyond fat, it suggests a lack of acidity. See also FAT

FLAT: Dull in flavor, low in acidity. Also, a sparkling wine that has lost its bubbles.

FLESHY: Smooth in texture and generous in flavor, with very little tannin. Opposite of THIN.

FLINTY: Tasting term for extremely dry white wines with a mineral flavor, whose bouquet suggests flint struck against steel.

FORTIFIED: Denotes a wine whose alcohol content has been increased by the addition of brandy or neutral spirits.

FOXY: Tasting term for the unique musky and grapey character of many native American varieties. Think Welch's grape juice.

FREE-RUN: The juice that escapes after the grape skins are crushed prior to pressing.

FRENCH OAK: Wine barrels coopered from oak grown in French forests, which impart vanilla, cedar and sometimes nutmeg or clove flavors.

FRUITY: Having the aroma and taste of fruit or fruits, but not necessarily sweet. Not a negative comment.

GEOGRAPHICAL INDICATION: Australia's hierarchy of appellations. The proposed outline dates from 1998 but the approval process was still under way at press time.

GRAND CRU: French, literally "great site," the top tier for specific vineyards in most regions that use the term. In Bordeaux, it is sub-sidiary to CRU CLASSÉ.

GRAPEY: Denotes the simple flavors and aromas of fresh table grapes, as opposed to the more complex fruit flavors (such as currant, black cherry, fig and apricot) found in fine wines.

GRASSY: Having the smell of fresh-mown grass, a signature descriptor for Sauvignon Blanc.

GREEN: Tasting of unripe fruit. Wines made from unripe grapes will often possess this quality. Pleasant if balanced with other flavors.

GRIP: A welcome firmness of tex-ture, usually from tannin and alco-hol, which helps give definition to wines such as Cabernet and Port.

GROWN, PRODUCED AND BOTTLED: On U.S. labels, means the winery handled everything from growing the grapes to bottling the wine.

HALF-BOTTLE: Holds 375 milli-liters.

HARD: Beyond FIRM; having so much acidity or tannin that the wine requires cellaring to be pleas-ant to drink.

HARMONIOUS: Tasting term that goes beyond BALANCED to sug-gest that all the elements work together to create a satisfying pattern.

HAZY: Tasting term for clarity that is not quite brilliant, but not cloudy either.

HEARTY: Tasting term for the full, warm quality of red wines with lots of alcohol and simple flavor. See also ROBUST, RUSTIC.

HEADY: Tasting term for high-alcohol wines.

HERBACEOUS: Often used to denote the taste and smell of herbs in a wine, though "herbal" is more grammatical. A plus in many wines such as Sauvignon Blanc, and to a lesser extent Merlot and Cabernet.

HOLLOW: Tasting term for a wine with a first taste and a short finish, and not much in the middle. (Wags calls such wines "donuts.")

HOT: High alcohol can seem to burn with "heat" on the finish. Acceptable in Port-style wines.

IMPERIAL: An oversized bottle holding 6 liters; the equivalent of eight standard bottles.

JEROBOAM: An oversized bottle holding the equivalent of six bottles. In Champagne, a jeroboam holds four bottles.

KOSHER: Wines made according to Jewish dietary law, supervised by a rabbi. Any type of wine can be kosher, including some Bordeaux châteaus, although the term has most commonly been associated with sweet wines made from Concord grapes.

LATE HARVEST: On U.S. labels, indicates that a wine was made from grapes picked riper (i.e, higher in sugar) than usual. Usually associ-ated with sweet wines.

LEAN: Tasting term for wines made in an austere style. The oppo-site of FLESHY

LEES: Sediment that collects in a barrel or tank during fermentation.

White wine is often aged "on its lees." See also SUR LIE.

LEGS: The viscous droplets that form and trickle down the inside of a glass when a wine is swirled. Formed by alcohol.

LENGTH: The amount of time the sensations of taste and aroma persist after swallowing. The longer the better. See also FINISH

LIMOUSIN: A forest near Limoges, France, that produces oak for barrels. See also FRENCH OAK

LIVELY: Fresh and fruity, with noticeable acidity.

LUSH: Tasting term for sweet wines that are especially soft or viscous.

MACERATION: Steeping the grape skins and solids in the wine after fermentation, when alcohol acts as a solvent to extract color, tannin and aroma from the skins. Cold maceration occurs before fermentation.

MADE AND BOTTLED BY: On U.S. labels, indicates only that the winery crushed, fermented and bottled a minimum of 10 percent of the wine in the bottle.

MADERIZED: Describes the brownish color and slightly sweet, somewhat caramelized and often nutty character found in mature dessert-style wines such as Madeira.

MAGNUM: An oversized bottle that holds 1.5 liters, the equivalent of two bottles.

MALIC ACID: One of the acids in grapes, especially prevalent in unripe grapes. It is also the predominant acid in green apples, and can impart a green apple-like flavor to the wine.

MALOLACTIC FERMENTATION: A natural process that converts malic acid into softer lactic acid and carbon dioxide, thus softening the wine and adding complexity

MATURE: Ready to drink.

MEATY: Red wines that show plenty of concentration and a chewy quality, and may even have an aroma of cooked meat.

MERCAPTANS: A class of chemicals that imparts to wine a stink reminiscent of bottled gas or a fart.

MERITAGE: Rhymes with "heritage". California vintners invented this term for their Bordeaux-style red and white blended wines. For reds, the grapes allowed are Cabernet Sauvignon, Merlot, Cabernet Franc, Petite Verdot and Malbec; for whites, Sauvignon Blanc and Sémillon.

MÉTHODE CHAMPENOISE: The traditional method for making high-quality sparkling wine, in which the secondary fermentation occurs inside the bottle. Required in Champagne. See also CHARMAT.

METHUSELAH: An extra-large bottle for Champagne holding 6 liters; the equivalent of eight standard bottles.

MUST: The unfermented juice of grapes before it is converted into wine.

MUSTY: Having an off-putting moldy or mildewy smell. The result of a wine being made from moldy grapes, stored in improperly cleaned tanks and barrels, or contaminated by a poor cork.

NEBUCHADNEZZAR: A giant Champagne bottle holding 15 liters; the equivalent of 20 standard bottles.

NÉGOCIANT (NÉGOCIANT-ELEVEUR): A French wine merchant who buys grapes and vinifies them (or buys wines and combines them), bottles the result under his own label and ships them. Particularly found in Burgundy. Two well-known examples are Joseph Drouhin and Louis Jadot.

NEVERS: Pronounced *Nay-vairh*, a forest in France that produces oak for barrels.

NONVINTAGE: Blended from more than one year's grapes. Many Champagnes and sparkling wines, and most Sherry and Port, are nonvintage.

NOSE: Tasting term comprising *aroma* and *bouquet*. Sometimes perceived as a snotty term (if you'll pardon the pun).

NOUVEAU: Light, fruity red wine bottled and sold as soon as possible after fermentation, meant to be drunk up quickly. Applies mostly to Beaujolais.

NUTTY: If a wine smells like nuts, it can be the result of exotic fermentations or just plain oxidation. Expected in fortified wines.

OAKY: A tasting term suggesting that the flavors imparted by oak barrel-aging predominate.

OFF-DRY: Indicates a slightly sweet wine in which sugar is barely perceptible, usually 0.6 percent to 1.4 percent residual sugar.

OXIDIZED: Tasting term for overlong exposure to air, resulting in a brownish color, lack of freshness and a suggestion of Sherry or old apples. Oxidized wines are also called maderized.

pH: A chemical measure of acidity or alkalinity, often used on wine labels from technical-minded wineries. The lower the pH the

tarter the wine. Most wines range from 3.0 to 3.7.

PHYLLOXERA: Tiny root lice that attack *Vitis vinifera* roots, eventually killing the vine. The disease was widespread in both Europe and California during the late 19th century, and returned to California in the 1980s.

PLUSH: One step beyond FLESHY

PRESS WINE (or PRESSING): The juice extracted after normal pressing for white wines and after fermentation for reds. Press wine has a deeper color and often more tannins than FREE-RUN juice. Wineries often blend a portion of press wine back into the main cuvée for backbone.

RESERVE, RESERVA, RISERVA: Legal terms used in Europe for wines that have been aged longer than other bottlings. Often sold at commensurately higher prices, though not always better. The term has no legal definition on U.S. labels, whether as reserve, private reserve, proprietor's reserve or any other variation. Some U.S. producers use it for their highest quality wines, others for their lowest.

PRODUCED AND BOTTLED BY: Indicates that the winery crushed, fermented and bottled at least 75 percent of the wine in the bottle.

PUNT: The dimple or indentation in the bottom of a bottle, originally meant to strengthen handblown glass containers; now mostly for show, except in sparkling wine bottles.

QUINTA: Pronounced *KEEN-ta*. Portuguese designation for a single vineyard.

RACKING: Moving wine by hose from one container to another,

leaving sediment behind. For aeration or clarification.

RACY: Tasting term for pleasantly high acidity and bright flavors.

RAW: Young and undeveloped, often tannic; typical of red wine sampled from barrel.

REDUCED: Wine that has not been exposed to air can develop stinky aromas due to reductive chemical reactions (as opposed to oxidation). Off aromas usually dissipate after exposure to air.

REHOBOAM: Oversized Champagne bottle holding 4.5 liters, equivalent to six regular bottles.

RESIDUAL SUGAR: Unfermented grape sugar in a finished wine.

ROOTSTOCK: Disease-resistant native American grapevine grown specifically to provide a root system on which to graft VITIS VINIFERA varieties. Most of the world uses this system to prevent attacks of PHYLLOXERA.

ROUND: Describes a texture that is smooth, not coarse or tannic.

RUSTIC: Tasting term for wines made by old-fashioned methods or tasting like wines made in an earlier era. Usually coarse and earthy, sometimes simple and fruity.

SALMANAZAR: An oversized Champagne bottle holding 9 liters, the equivalent of 12 bottles.

SECOND LABEL: Estate wineries often bottle excess production, lesser wines or purchased wines under a label other than the one that made them famous, often at a lower price.

SOMMELIER: Pronounced *so-mel-YEA*. In a restaurant, the server responsible for wine. Often this is a manager who buys wine, organizes the wine list, maintains the cellar and ultimately negotiates the sale of wine to customers.

SOFT: Describes wines low in acid, made for easy drinking. Opposite of HARD.

SPICY: Tasting term for flavors such as anise, cinnamon, clove, nutmeg and pepper, often present in complex wines.

STALKY, STEMMY: Tasting terms for an unpleasant greenness and astringency from too-long fermentation with the grape stems.

STRUCTURE: The combined effect of elements such as acidity, tannin, glycerin, alcohol and sugar as they relates to a wine's texture. Usually preceded by a modifier, as in "firm structure" or "lacking in structure."

SULFITES: Winemakers all over the world use sulfur dioxide to clean equipment, kill unwanted organisms in the wine and protect finished wines from spoilage. A small amount remains in the bottle, and U.S. label laws require a statement to announce its presence. Those highly sensitive to sulfites know it and should avoid wine.

SUPPLE: Tasting term for smooth texture, mostly in reds, not quite SOFT.

SUR LIE: Pronounced *suhr lee*, French for "on the lees." Denotes white wines kept in contact with dead yeast cells after fermentation and not racked or otherwise filtered. This procedure is a normal part of fermenting red wine. Used in Burgundy, Muscadet, Alsace and Germany, now copied in the New World to add complexity. Like anything else, it can be overdone.

SWEET: In tasting terms, most people begin to perceive sweetness at concentrations of 0.3 to 0.7 percent.

TANNIN: A mouth-puckering substance derived primarily from grape skins, seeds and stems, but also from oak barrels. Tannin acts as a natural preservative that helps wine age and develop. Too much tannin can be bitter, and feels like tea brewed overlong.

TART: Sharp-tasting because of acidity; usually meant as a positive.

TARTARIC ACID: The principal acid in wine.

TARTRATES: Harmless crystals of potassium bitartrate that may form in cask or bottle (often on the cork) from the tartaric acid naturally present in wine.

TIGHT: Describes a wine in which all the elements have not softened, but the texture is not too HARD.

TIRED: Limp, feeble, lackluster. Opposite of FRESH

TOASTY: Literally reminiscent of lightly burnt toast, complete with the bready notes. A characteristic that often develops in dry sparkling wines.

VEGETAL: A general tasting term. As FRUITY is to berry, cherry and apricot, VEGETAL is to bell pepper, celery and asparagus. Not often desirable except as a grace note.

VINICULTURE: The science or study of grape production for wine and the making of wine.

VINOUS: A tasting term for dull wines lacking in distinct character. Literally means "winelike."

VINTAGE: The year a wine was made, determined by when the grapes were harvested. Also refers to the time of year in which the harvest takes place. ("I'm going to Bordeaux for the vintage.") See also NONVINTAGE.

VINTED BY: Has no legal meaning.

VINTNER: Literally a wine merchant, but generally used to mean a wine producer or winery proprietor.

VITICULTURAL AREA: In the U.S., a legally defined grape-growing region (also known as AMERICAN VITICULTURAL AREA, OR A.V.A.). See also APPELLATION.

VITICULTURE: The cultivation, science and study of grapes.

VITIS VINIFERA: Pronounced *VIT-is vin-IF-era*. Classic European wine-making grapevines, such as Cabernet Sauvignon and Chardonnay. Native American grapevines such as *Vitis labrusca*, which includes Concord, make wines with very different flavors and are not considered fine.

VOLATILE (or Volatile Acidity): Describes an excessive and undesirable amount of ACETIC ACID, which gives a wine a sour, vinegary edge.

YEAST: Micro-organisms that act on sugar to convert it into alcohol and carbon dioxide, a process known as fermentation. The predominant wine yeast, *saccharomyces cerevisiae*, is the same one that ferments beer and makes bread dou gh rise.

Index

I n d e x

Photo Credits

Fred Seidman: pp. 64-65, 74-75, 146 (top & bottom)

J.L. Smith: p. 218

Courtesy of Sotheby's: p. 101

Tim Stead: p. 59

Liz Steger: pp. 122, 127, 129, 130, 132, 133, 204

Harvey Steiman: pp. 98-99

James Suckling: pp. 32, 72-73

Rachel Weill: p. 183

Brian Whitney: p. 137

Courtney Grant Winston: p. 102

Steve Wisbauer: p. 126 (top left)

Jon Wyand: pp. 16, 21, 22, 161

Arnold Zahn/Blackstar: p. 117

Edited by Ann Berkhausen and Amy Lyons

Designed by Liz Trovato

Cover design by Bill Jones